REMARRIAGE

FAMILY STUDIES TEXT SERIES

Series Editor: RICHARD J. GELLES, *University of Rhode Island*
Series Associate Editor: ALEXA A. ALBERT, *University of Rhode Island*

This series of textbooks is designed to examine topics relevant to a broad view of family studies. The series is aimed primarily at undergraduate students of family sociology and family relations, among others. Individual volumes will be useful to students in psychology, home economics, counseling, human services, social work, and other related fields. Core texts in the series cover such subjects as theory and conceptual design, research methods, family history, cross-cultural perspectives, and life course analysis. Other texts will cover traditional topics, such as dating and mate selection, parenthood, divorce and remarriage, and family power. Topics that have been receiving more recent public attention will also be dealt with, including family violence, later life families, and fatherhood.

Because of their wide range and coverage, Family Studies Texts can be used singly or collectively to supplement a standard text or to replace one. These books will be of interest to both students and professionals in a variety of disciplines.

Volumes in this series:

1. LATER LIFE FAMILIES, Timothy H. Brubaker

2. INTIMATE VIOLENCE IN FAMILIES,
   Richard J. Gelles & Claire Pedrick Cornell

3. BECOMING A PARENT, Ralph LaRossa

4. FAMILY RESEARCH METHODS, Brent C. Miller

5. PATHS TO MARRIAGE, Bernard I. Murstein

6. WORK AND FAMILY LIFE, Patricia Voydanoff

7. REMARRIAGE, Marilyn Ihinger-Tallman & Kay Pasley

Volumes planned for this series:

THEORIES OF FAMILY LIFE, David M. Klein
FAMILY POWER, Maximiliane Szinovacz
FAMILY STRESS, Pauline Boss
DIVORCE, Sharon J. Price & Patrick C. McKenry
CONCEPTUAL FRAMEWORKS FOR FAMILY STUDIES, Keith Farrington
THE SINGLE PARENT FAMILY, Alexa A. Albert
FAMILIES AND HEALTH, William Doherty & Thomas Campbell
PARENT-CHILD RELATIONSHIPS, Gary W. Peterson & Greer Litton Fox

Marilyn Ihinger-Tallman
and
Kay Pasley

REMARRIAGE

FAMILY STUDIES
TEXT SERIES 7

For information address:

SAGE Publications, Inc.
2111 West Hillcrest Drive
Newbury Park, California 91320

SAGE Publications Inc.   SAGE Publications Ltd.
275 South Beverly Drive  28 Banner Street
Beverly Hills   London EC1Y 8QE
California 90212   England

SAGE PUBLICATIONS India Pvt. Ltd.
M-32 Market
Greater Kailash I
New Delhi 110 048 India

Printed in the United States of America

Library of Congress Cataloging-in-Publication Data

Main entry under title:

Ihinger-Tallman, Marilyn.
    Remarriage.

    (Family studies text series ; 7)
    Includes bibliographies and indexes.
    1. Remarriage.   2. Stepfamilies.   I. Pasley, Kay.
II. Title.   III. Series: Family studies text series ;
v. 7.
HQ1018.I36   1987   306.8′4   87-4713
ISBN 0-8039-2628-6
ISBN 0-8039-2629-4 (pbk.)

To RRW   *Because we see the same beauty*
in the world.
KP

For Irv and Robert
Lance
Shannon
Phillip and
Erika

Because your love, encouragement,
and just being help me to
reach further than I can grasp.
MIT

Contents

Preface

THE SLIM VOLUME you hold in your hands is intended to convey as much information as is available about remarriage and stepparenting. Gathering that information was not as difficult as it would have been had we elected to focus on another family topic. This is because remarriage and stepparenting have only recently captured the interest of family scholars; the field is relatively new.

When the divorce rate began to climb in the mid-1960s it was—and still is—accompanied by a high remarriage rate. For remarried adults who have no children, the marriage experience is probably not too different from that of first-married couples. However, the majority of remarrying couples do bring at least one child from a previous union to their new marriage. These couples face a unique challenge, one that involves creating a "family" with a new and distinct identity from the one or ones they lived in before. Both adults and children in a stepfamily bring with them memories, expectations, and behaviors that were developed in another family "culture." These may slow the development of a new family identity. Also, the children may not feel positive about being a part of a new family, and may wish very much to have the old one back.

For the majority of remarried families the difficulties associated with establishing a new and stable family unit are not surmountable. This is evident in a redivorce rate of about 60%—a figure slightly higher than the 50% divorce rate for first-married couples (Glick, 1984). The pages that follow spell out in some detail the many ways that remarriage is different from first marriage. Although we focus on some of the problems of remarriage, we also attempt to call attention to the processes of adjustment and the strengths of remarriage and stepfamily life.

The book is organized in the following way. A short introductory chapter calls attention to the key features that make second (or subsequent) marriages distinct from first marriages. In Chapter 2 we present a historical account of how remarriage in our time differs from earlier eras. This chapter also reports the different rates of remarriage for males and females, blacks and whites, and for people with different levels of education and income. Chapter 3 identifies several important family processes associated with marriage and shows why these processes are more complicated in remarriage. Several "types" of remarriages have been identified and they are described and analyzed in this chapter. The effects of cohabitation on remarriage are examined in Chapter 4. This chapter also compares marital satisfaction between first-married and remarried couples and discusses the difficulties couples face when they merge two households. Chapter 5 describes the problems and satisfactions that remarried couples experience when one or both partners bring children into the new marriage. Here, too, we explore how remarriage and stepfamily life affects children's development. In Chapter 6 we consider the problematic nature of the stepparent-stepchild relationship and sibling and stepsibling relationships. We also report on how involvement with friends and extended kin influences stepfamily life. Chapter 7 reviews the advice offered to remarrieds. We discuss some approaches to enhancing stepfamily development and examine public policy issues. The final chapter could be viewed as an Appendix. It focuses on research and emphasizes why we must be cautious about interpreting the findings from the early studies on remarriage and stepparenting. This chapter calls attention to the special methodological problems facing scholars who study this topic.

We have included several discussion questions at the end of every chapter, as well as suggestions for further reading. The questions are intended to get the reader thinking about and beyond the specific content offered in the book. The related readings can help readers pursue their interest in the topics covered in the chapter. These readings consist of both scholarly and popular writings on remarriage and stepfamilies.

Like many social scientists, our interest in this particular subject was sparked from our experiences with stepfamilies and our interest in the changing nature of the American family. This book is not a how-to-make-a-remarriage-work volume. Rather, we have tried to produce a text that reviews and reports as objectively (and as interestingly) as possible what the available research and theory have to say about remarriage and stepfamilies.

Acknowledgments

AS WE CONCLUDED our writing task, our indebtedness to many others became increasingly obvious. First, we are grateful to the several anonymous reviewers and to Rich Gelles and Alexa Albert, the two coeditors of this miniseries, for their helpful evaluations. These folks did not hesitate to call our attention to first-draft problems, but softened their critiques with enough positive feedback to keep us writing. Because our reviewers were all professors (we think) and beyond the age of our younger readers, we are especially grateful to Rob, Peg, Shannon, and Erika who reacted honestly to their mom's request for feedback ("that's boring"; "give us Dear Abby's answers"; "Workman's compensation is a sexist term"; "What's the point of this section?"). We are thankful, also, to John Crosby and Jerry Bigner for their comments on an early version. And finally, thanks to Irv for his forever willingness to read another draft. The credit for much of the technical and tedious work of editing disks, typing the bibliography, and printing and xeroxing numerous copies at a moment's notice that was necessary to get this volume "out the door" on time goes to Dorothy Casavant, with help from Ruth Self and Anne Lewandowski. We are indeed appreciative for their unflagging goodwill and eagerness to help, and their extreme competence in doing so. We want to thank the very special men and women in Spokane County who participated in our study on remarriage. Their cooperation and willingness to help provided many insights into remarriage and stepparenting. We want to acknowledge the many colleagues with whom professional dialogues and intellectual exchanges about remarriage and stepfamilies have kept us stimulated and hopeful that these topics will get the research attention they deserve. We especially want to recognize the members of the S.R.C.D. study group on remarriage and stepfamilies: Connie Ahrons, Glenn Clingempeel, Marilyn Coleman, Frank Furstenberg, Jr., Larry Ganong, E. Mavis Hetherington, and Doris Jacobson. Jean Giles-Sims, Margaret Crosbie-Burnett, and Emily and John Visher are also valued colleagues in our mutual endeavors.

CHAPTER
1

How Are Remarriages Different?

Dear Abby: Please settle a giant family dispute. Is your mother's or father's new spouse your stepfather or stepmother only if you are living with them? You are the only one who can settle this, so please put your answer in the paper as soon as possible. (C. J. in Newport Beach)

Dear Abby: I have a question I hope you can answer. My dad was married three times.

With wife No. 1, he had a son.

With wife No. 2, he had two daughters.

With wife No. 3, he had me.

What relation are his son and daughters to me—stepbrother and step-sisters? Or half-brother and half-sister? Would wife No. 2 and wife No. 3 be his son's stepmothers? Would wives No. 1 and 2 be any relation to me? (All Screwed Up in Ohio)

—from "Dear Abby" column by Abigail Van Buren, © 1985 Universal Press Syndicate. Reprinted with permission. All rights reserved.

MANY OF YOU will read this book simply because it is required as part of a course. Others may fulfill an assignment, and also be eager to find out about a type of family that is part of your own personal experience. You're likely not as ignorant as C. J. in Newport Beach or All Screwed Up in Ohio,[1] but you may have wondered why your friend hated her stepparent so much that she ran away from home, or what it is like to spend all summer in another state, living with a parent you only see once a year. Or maybe you wonder if you and your stepmother will ever get along. This book will not be able to answer these specific questions because they pertain to you, a particular individual. However, it will shed some light on what is happening in some remarriages and step-families across the country, as reported by researchers and clinicians who study and work with these families.

One of the conclusions stemming from this body of literature is that there is some confusion about step-kin terminology and relationships. This is illustrated by the appeals to Dear Abby to help people define their steprelationships. However, there are other sources of confusion associated with remarriage besides knowing the right terminology or correct relationship to a parent's former spouse. The issue of what to call these new relatives is a problem for some. Is a new stepfather "dad" simply because your mother decided to remarry? Many people wonder how to behave toward strangers who suddenly become family. There are few rules that define how to interact with a new stepparent, stepgrandparent, or stepsister. Sociologist Andrew Cherlin (1978) proposed a hypothesis that called remarriage an "incomplete institution." He was describing the situation we have outlined earlier—namely, that there are few norms or rules to define the expected behaviors associated with remarriage and stepfamily life. The hypothesis is that this ambiguity results in confusion, uncertainty, and ultimately divorce among remarried couples. In this volume we try to describe the sources of the confusion and ambiguity. We explore the problematic aspects, as well as the unique strengths, associated with remarriage and stepfamilies. This first chapter begins by acquainting you with the specific ways that first marriage differs from second, or subsequent, marriage.

CHARACTERISTICS THAT DISTINGUISH
FIRST MARRIAGE FROM REMARRIAGE

Childless Remarriage

A remarriage that takes place between two adults who are childless is different from a first marriage in only a few ways. One of the most important of these is the fact that one or both partners already has the experience of having been married. Such experience is sometimes problematic for the new couple. A source of difficulty can be the continuing relationship between ex-spouses and/or ex-inlaws. Doris Jacobson, a professor of social welfare, describes such a situation:

> She is unreasonable. Sometimes I just want to talk to Jane (my former wife) about old times. After all, we went through high school together, know a lot of the same people. It is nice to get together sometimes. I miss the old talks. But Nancy [current wife] raises hell when she knows I have been there and stayed. I think she is not reasonable. We fight about this a lot [1980: 40].

In this situation the second wife's anger and jealousy is fueled by the continuing attachment her husband has to a person with whom he once shared an intimate relationship. The conflict comes because he sees nothing wrong with maintaining this friendship. It is possible that similar feelings of jealousy may be generated over an old boyfriend, girlfriend, or lover, but we believe that a former marriage produces more intense feelings—marriage implies a more intimate relationship and commitment. Adults differ in the degree to which they work through the loss and grief that results from ending a marriage (Bitterman, 1967; Weiss, 1975). In this example, the husband has no desire to give up one kind of attachment to his former wife. That knowledge is a source of distress to his current wife. Jacobson sums up the situation as follows: "The extent to which the . . . marital separation or divorce has been adaptively resolved prior to the remarriage will affect interaction between the new marital partners" (1980: 39). However, we have very little reliable data on the resolution process and the nature of the continuing psychological attachment between former spouses (Kressel, 1985).

Sociologists Frank Furstenberg and Graham Spanier (1984) identify four specific reasons remarriage differs from first marriage. One of these reflects Jacobson's ideas. The two sociologists call attention to the fact of a prior spouse and the possibility of a continuing need to interact with that person, especially if there are children in the family. A second reason marriage and remarriage are different relates to the point we made at the beginning of this section regarding the experience of being married before. Both behaviorally and psychologically, a first marriage provides a baseline from which to judge the second marriage. A remarried spouse is likely to compare the former relationship with his or her current situation and be more or less satisfied. The third reason is that first and second marriages take place at different times in the individual's life course. If there are a number of years spent in a first marriage before it ends in divorce or death, changes will have occurred in a person's level of maturity, his or her life experiences, and economic and social status. Because of these changes, the circumstances under which the second marriage occurs are quite different. Marriage is quite likely to be viewed differently the second time. The final reason suggested by these writers for the differences between first marriages and remarriages is that remarried persons are members of two different marriage *cohorts*. (A cohort is a group of people that have something in common; they share the same birth year, or birth decade, they graduated from the same high school class, and so on.) Thus for two different marriage cohorts the rules and expectations for behavior may be quite different. For example, societal expectations about household tasks have changed considerably in two decades. The expectations for a woman marrying in 1955 were that she would accept a traditional role and assume primary responsibility for maintaining the home. If this woman divorced and remarried in 1975, when greater equality between marriage partners was being espoused, she would likely approach marriage roles differently in her second marriage. Such societal norms compel remarriage partners to rethink marriage according to contemporary standards.

These are the primary ways that remarriages differ from first marriages when only adults are involved in the promise and commitment to share a life together. The situation becomes more problematic when one or both spouses brings a child or children into the remarriage. We consider this type of remarriage next.

Remarriages with Children

The inclusion of children from a former marriage complicates and can aggravate the process of adjustment to a new marriage. Not only are there the differences outlined earlier, but the presence of children from a prior marriage differentiates stepfamilies from first families. One group of writers (Sager et al., 1980) has identified several of these characteristics. These features are important to the discussion in future chapters, so they are briefly elaborated here.

(1) *When children are involved the family is created anew, without the gradual addition of new members through pregnancy and birth.* This means that although two adults may fall in love and decide to spend the rest of their life together, the children in the family may be barely acquainted with their new stepparent. Loving, liking, and respect between stepparent and stepchild may not be fully developed by the time the marriage takes place.

(2) *A remarriage may take place at a time when the necessities and tasks of the family life cycle are incompatible with the needs and tasks of the individual.* An example of this situation would be the experience of an older man who, soon after marrying a much younger woman, suddenly gains custody of his teenage sons and they come to live with the newly married couple. One of the tasks at the early stage of marriage is to develop and strengthen the bonds of intimacy between spouses. In any marriage the inclusion of an infant or young child can hinder this process. The inclusion of young adolescent males who are only a few years younger than the new wife is sure to make this task more problematic.

(3) *An ex-spouse and ex-grandparents may have input to the new family system — input that may not be welcomed by the remarried spouses.* The boundaries that all families must maintain to establish and protect their privacy and autonomy are vulnerable because former family

members have some legitimate claim on at least the child in the family. For this reason they can justify input that may not be welcome.

(4) *Feelings of mixed allegiance and guilt may be created in adults and children as a result of their past family experience.* Spouses may have feelings of mixed allegiance and guilt toward their children and ex-spouses. They may be concerned that they are not giving them enough money, time, or attention. Children, too, may have feelings of conflicting loyalty or allegiance toward parent and stepparent, or between other family and stepfamily members.

(5) *The presence of children increases the permeability of family boundaries.* When children belong to two households, they can travel back and forth between them. They may carry messages ("Dad bought a new Mercedes") or behave in inappropriate ways for either or both biological parents.

(6) *Children may not want to be part of the family.* Children rarely have a voice in the decision to remarry, and thus they resemble a "captive audience" in a stepfamily. When a child does not want to be part of the family, he or she can act in ways that make life miserable for other family members.

(7) *Children may suffer psychologically from parental divorce or death of a parent.* Some children may be scarred emotionally by intense marital conflict or from having experienced physical desertion by one or both parents. The separation-divorce-remarriage transition does result in long-term psychological difficulties for a few children. However, most studies show that very few children suffer long-term trauma from the experience. However, subtle psychological consequences, such as a decrease in the level of trust of others or hostility toward one or the other sex, may occur that are difficult or impossible to measure.

(8) *There is role confusion for all remarried family members—parents, stepparents, and children.* This characteristic reflects Cherlin's incomplete institution hypothesis and explains why people write to the Dear Abby column for information about steprelations. Members in first-married families usually know what is expected of them. Stepfathers may know what good fathering means to them, but their ideas and expectations may be quite different from both the ideas and expectations of their stepchildren.

We shall have occasion to refer to each of these eight points at various places throughout the book. By listing them here we hope to sensitize you to the unique circumstances of remarriage that are ultimately the source of many of the problems remarried couples face.

PROCLIVITY TOWARD MARRIAGE

The term *conjugal succession* has been used by sociologist Furstenberg (1982) to describe the pattern of marriage-divorce-remarriage found in the United States today. (In 1950 Paul Landis referred to the same phenomena as *sequential polygamy,* and Margaret Mead coined the term *serial monogamy*). In the next chapter we will detail the history and related statistics associated with this marital succession. Here we want to call attention to one central idea that underlies conjugal succession: the marriage-oriented behavior of Americans.

In the United States, as in most of the world, the family has responsibility for reproduction and for the initial socialization and care of the children born into that family unit. The traditional (ideal) pattern in the United States has been to choose a marriage partner with the promise of living a lifetime together, until the death of one partner. Additionally, the traditional pattern has been to bring children into that union and raise them to adulthood.

During the past two decades, demographers have charted two trends that indicate some shifts or changes in these traditional living arrangements and the ways that children are parented. One of these trends is reflected in the growing number of children born to unmarried mothers. The second trend is the central theme of this book: the tendency for increasing numbers of adults to voluntarily dissolve a first marriage and yet be ready to enter into a second one, or even a third, fourth, or fifth. As we discuss the topic of remarriage and present the data related to it, we are not saying the first-marriage family is "dead." Nor are we advocating any new family system. Rather, our intent is to call attention to the change that is taking place regarding marriage and remarriage patterns, to inform you of the behaviors that are associated with it, and to try to help you understand the implications it may have for adults and children growing up in the midst of it. To quote the well-known demographer Paul Glick (1984: 24):

> Despite increases in divorce, lone parenting, and life long single status, most people will continue to live in a family, though the family may not be the same as it is today. Although American households continue to change, family ties will remain.

In summary, this chapter began by pointing out the ways that first marriage differs from remarriage; several characteristics differentiating them were discussed. These characteristics will be the subject of the chapters that follow. Attention was called to the trends that portray Americans as being marriage-oriented, with a proclivity to marry, divorce, and remarry. However, marriage-oriented though we may be, the divorce rate after remarriage remains high.

DISCUSSION QUESTIONS

(1) What is Cherlin's incomplete institution hypothesis? What might underly the awkwardness or feelings of discomfort people have when interacting with brand new step-kin?

(2) How might the experience of having been previously married influence a new marriage? Give examples.

(3) Consider the four factors mentioned by Furstenberg and Spanier and the eight characteristics related to children in remarriages. How might they influence the adjustment of family members to remarriage?

(4) What is meant by conjugal succession? What are some possible consequences of conjugal succession for families in America?

(5) Why do you think that Americans value the marriage institution so highly that they will marry two, three, or more times? What needs does marriage satisfy?

RELATED READINGS

CHERLIN, A. (1978) "Remarriage as an incomplete institution." American Journal of Sociology 84: 634-650.

VISHER, E. and J. VISHER (1983) "Stepparenting: blending families," pp. 133-146 in H. I. McCubbin and C. R. Figley (eds.) Stress and the Family, vol. I: Coping with Normative Transitions. New York: Brunner/Mozel.

NOTE

1. Are you curious about Abby's answers? She told C. J., "A stepmother is the wife of one's father by a subsequent marriage, and a stepfather is the husband of one's mother by a subsequent marriage. The relationship remains the same whether you live with them or not." To All Screwed Up she wrote, "The son and two daughters of your father are your half-brother and half-sisters. Wives No. 1 and No. 2 would be no relation to you. But wife No. 2 would be the former stepmother of your half-brother, and your real mother would be his stepmother."

CHAPTER
2

History and Demographics

In populations of the past, life was short. And, just because life was short, . . . it was possible to envisage life-long marriage. The termination of a marriage through death of one of the spouses was a disaster for members of the household who were faced with possible extinction. Thus, remarriage may be regarded as the first line of defense, entered into in order to safeguard the continued existence of the surviving members of the household [Sogner and Dupaquier, 1981: 3].

A badly run farm either lacks a woman, or is run by a woman.
                                                    —Scandinavian Folk Saying

CHAPTER 1 INDICATED that marriage practices in the United States are changing. This chapter will document these changes in greater detail. We want to put marriage and remarriage into a historical perspective to expand your view of this change. It is easier to understand current social change if you have an understanding of changes that have taken place in the past. Before we turn to history, however, two concepts need to be defined. When we write about the *remarriage rate*, we are refering to the percentage of all persons who marry who are contracting a remarriage. Another concept is important for your understanding of the material in this chapter. On several occasions we use the term *sex ratio*. This is a calculation of the number of males for every 100 females.

In the following sections we describe how rates of remarriage, and behavior related to remarriage, changed over time. We show how attitude and custom differed according to both culture and time period. These behavioral variations were the result of economic conditions and complex cultural patterns.

REMARRIAGE IN EUROPE: THE MIDDLE AGES

Attitudes and Custom

The Middle Ages was the historical period that formed our Western attitudes toward marriage and remarriage (Dupaquier et al., 1981). Recent historical/demographic studies conducted in England, France, and other European countries show that remarriage was both frequent and widespread during the Middle Ages. However, several shifts in attitude about remarriage emerge as we piece together information that describes practices of the past. Most reports place the remarriage rate at 20% - 30%, depending on the sex of the bereaved spouse and the particular historical time and place studied. At the same time, there is some evidence that remarriage was disapproved of in different times and places.

Although admitting that there is scant evidence to back his interpretation, the French historian Philippe Aries (1981) concluded that remarriage was generally disapproved of by the Western Catholic church prior to the eighth century. This was in spite of the fact that remarriage was commonly practiced. Marriage and remarriage were subject to ecclesiastical law, but custom and practice associated with marriage and remarriage remained independent of church doctrine. Marriage was a private act, subject to the constraints, custom, and opinions of the *community*, not the church. The priest was asked to give the church's blessing to the bedchamber, the bed, and the bride, principally as a precaution, not because it was necessary. As an example of the church's disapproval, Aries cites the refusal to pronounce the nuptial benediction over widows who remarried—a benediction that was not refused widowers who took a virgin as a second wife.

Approval of remarriage increased around the twelfth or thirteenth century as the church began to grant widows and widowers the right to remarry, even though remarriage had been a frequent practice all along. This was a time when the church was expanding its role in the regulation of marriage. In many places there were differences between first and second marriage ceremonies. For example, first marriages were the occasion for a village celebration. The daytime ceremony was festive, with food, drink, and merriment. Remarried couples, on the other hand, married at night without the benediction of the church.

By the end of the Middle Ages the climate changed again. There is some indication that the remarriage of widows (but not widowers) was disapproved of. Pejorative terms for stepmothers were introduced into the common vocabulary in Italy and France.

The French and Italian practice of *charivaris* exemplifies this change in attitude and the community's hostility to a widow remarrying. *Charivaris* is translated as "rough music." It was a custom whereby the young and unmarried males of the village (but others often joined in) harassed the remarried couple with noise, insults, and even barricades. Historian Natalie Davis (1975) reports that masked youths would assemble outside the cottage of the newly remarried couple at night and bang pots, tambourines, bells, and horns, sometimes for as long as a week. Especially when there was a big difference between the ages of the couple, there would be loud, mocking laughter, cries of *"Vieille carcasse, folle d'amour"* (old carcass, crazy with love). The couple sometimes redeemed themselves for having deprived the villagers of the food and money of a traditional wedding by paying a "fine" of three times the wedding costs. Sometimes in order to avoid this, the widowed woman and her chosen partner would give a party on the day they posted their banns in Church. Everyone in the village was invited, except the bride and groom. The party was not to celebrate the coming wedding, but to allay the hostility and the protests of the villagers.

There were several reasons for the hostility expressed by the community. First, the traditional marriage ceremony celebrated the fertility or "procreative career" of the couple; a second or subsequent marriage did not usually serve the function of reproduction. Second, very frequently remarriage meant that a young never-married female or male was taken from the pool of eligibles, limiting the choices of those not yet married. A third source of community disapproval stemmed from marriages between partners who were unequal in age, status, or wealth— an inequality that usually existed with remarriage. Jack Goody (1983) reminds us that the hostile reaction of the villagers was to the particular incident, not to the practice of remarriage. This was because family life was dependent on two adults, each of whom was responsible for different tasks to keep the household functioning smoothly. This is the meaning behind the Scandinavian folk saying quoted at the beginning of this chapter. A farm could not run without a woman nor could it be run by a woman alone.

The evidence is not clear whether the *charivaris* demonstration was limited to the remarriage of women. However, the church forbid *charivaris* against second marriages from the thirteenth century on. This did not mean the behavior stopped (Davis, 1975). During the sixteenth century another change in the attitude toward remarriage occurred. The significance of the *charivaris* ritual seems to have shifted from one of prohibition to one of compensation. The celebration was taken as a substitute for the remarriage ceremony.

Frequency of Remarriage

Evidence from sixteenth-century English marriage registers indicates the remarriage rate in England was between 25% and 30%. Also, the interval between marriages was short. Of the men who remarried, almost half (48%) did so within one year of widowhood, whereas 37% of the women remarried within one year (Schofield and Wrigley, 1981).

Remarriage was as frequent in France during the sixteenth and seventeenth centuries as in England. Between 20% and 33% of all marriages during this time included a bride or groom who was widowed. Here, too, length of widowhood was short—between 33% to 50% of widowers remarried within one year of the death of their spouse. Widowhood for women usually lasted a little longer, typically two years or more. The same rate of remarriage continued in France during the seventeenth and eighteenth centuries (Bideau, 1980).

During the late 1700s the remarriage rate was about 25% of all marriages in Iceland, but during times of crisis (famine, epidemics) the rate increased to as high as 40%. Here, too, the mourning period after bereavement was short. A widower could legally remarry six weeks after the death of his wife. A widow, however, would have to wait three months. This wait made sure that she was not pregnant by her deceased husband (Hansen, 1981).

Significant demographic changes affected remarriage patterns in the nineteenth century. In addition to a decrease in the number of children per family and a greater number of persons who never married, the death rate dropped significantly. This decrease in the death rate influenced the remarriage rate—it also decreased. Whereas the remarriage rate in Europe before 1650 amounted to 25%-30% of all marriages, it dropped to about 10% during the last part of the nineteenth century.

At this time previously accepted customs associated with remarriage were disapproved. For example, the short time period between death of spouse and remarriage was frowned upon. An older widow's marriage to a younger man was no longer readily tolerated.

These trends occurred throughout the Western world. Studies of remarriage in Italy, England, France, and Scandinavia, for example, report that the frequency of remarriage declined continuously during the second half of the nineteenth century. By the middle 1800s the rate of remarriage ranged from 10% in England and 11.8% in Italy, to between 13% and 14% in France (Bideau, 1980; Livi-Bacci, 1981; Schofield and Wrigley, 1981).

FACTORS THAT HASTENED OR INHIBITED REMARRIAGE IN WESTERN EUROPE

Several factors affected the rate of remarriage. The most important of these were the sex of surviving spouse, age at time of spouse's death, and presence and number of dependent children. Social class,

preference for a never-married versus a widowed person as a new partner, and urban versus rural residence were also factors associated
with remarriage.

We have already mentioned that men spent less time between marriages. They also remarried at a faster rate than women. The younger
a person was at the time of his or her spouse's death, the higher the
probability of remarriage. Presence and number of children seemed to
deter the remarriage of women, but findings are mixed for men. In
seventeenth- and eighteenth-century England and eighteenth- and
nineteenth-century Germany, the number of children was associated with
delayed remarriage for men. However, another study reporting seven-
teenth- and eighteenth-century data in England found men with children
tended to remarry quickly. This inconsistency might be because of
regional differences, or marriage market differences. The marriage market is discussed later on.

Some information on the influence of social class and remarriage
probabilities is available. Marriage and remarriage among persons
from the middle and upper classes in Protestant Germany (1550 to 1800)
show that members of these social groups (aldermen, clergymen,
mayors, judges, lawyers, university professors, headmasters, merchants,
and physicians) had a slightly longer interval between death of spouse
and remarriage than did the average city dweller. Higher class status
did not seem to benefit women in finding new spouses. Widows of the
middle and upper classes had no greater likelihood of remarrying than
the widow of average class status. This delay was in spite of the fact
that higher-class widowed women tended to be slightly younger and had
married at younger ages. These characteristics would be expected to
make them more, not less, desirable candidates for remarriage (Imhof,
1981). Demographers David Gaunt and Orvar Lofgren (1981) report
that in preindustrial Denmark remarriage rates varied by social class,
with farmers remarrying more frequently than the nobility or clergy.

There is some reason to think that an urban versus rural environment influenced remarriage probabilities. In sixteenth- and seventeenth-
century France remarriage was more common in towns than in the countryside (Cabourdin, 1981). In Italy in the first half of the nineteenth
century, remarriage also was reported to be more frequent in towns than
in the country (Bellettini, 1981). On the other hand, Alain Bideau (1980)
found no rural-urban differences in remarriage rates in France between
1670 and 1840.

The chances of widowed persons remarrying depended on more than
just their sex, age, children, class, or residence. Other social factors

played a role in creating remarriage probabilities. We call these marriage market factors.

The Marriage Market

The term *market* is a concept used to describe commercial activity whereby the exchange of commodities occurs. The term *marriage market* is a concept used to represent the activities by which marriages are negotiated or arranged.

Both cultural and natural (physical) barriers exist that inhibit the marriage market, making it more difficult to find marriage partners. For example, oceans and mountain ranges are natural barriers that restricted communication and travel in earlier times, limiting the pool of eligible partners. Similarly, religious restrictions, emigration, military conscriptions, wars, epidemics, famines, and the expansion of the economic and labor markets that influenced movement from the countryside into town all affected the size, structure, and mobility of the population from which (re)marriage partners were sought. In spite of the limited travel in the past, however, the operation of the marriage market was never confined to a single village. Many men and women contracted a second or subsequent marriage in a parish other than the one in which their first marriage ended. This could happen in a variety of ways. An older widow might move to another parish to live with an adult son or daughter after the death of her husband. There she competed in a new market. A merchant traveling to sell his wares might meet a woman in a distant district and bring her back to his home village as wife.

One thing the records of the past make clear is that in the marriage market the widowed competed with never-married persons for partners. During times of high mortality there were many more widowed men and women competing with the never married for spouses. Many younger, never-married persons preferred to marry a widow or widower rather than delay marriage. In the past, delaying marriage was often necessary because of the lack of sufficient economic resources—a precondition for marriage. Although "sufficient" changed in meaning over time, most young people had to wait until they had accumulated the material goods or landholding to afford a spouse. When marrying a person who had been married before, this wait was circumvented. During the Middle Ages no strong negative sanctions existed in communities against marriages between widowed and never-married persons (even the *charivaris* custom was only a temporary inconvenience) and even large age differences were acceptable. It did not go without consideration that a young person marrying an older widow or widower stood a good chance of remarrying again at a later date, often from a stronger economic position. Marriage to an older person sometimes provided the opportunity to learn the skills necessary for success. Solvi Sogner and Jacques Dupaquier (1981: 10) quote a young widower who said gratefully of his older deceased wife: "It was she who taught me how to do a man's work."

The sex ratio, as it existed at any given time, also had an important effect upon the marriage market. When there was a surplus of men, first and subsequent marriage rates for women were high. Conversely, when there was a surplus of women, many more women spent their lives unmarried, and fewer widows remarried.

When the age difference between spouses is a relevant factor in the mate selection process, demographers say there exists the potential of a *marriage squeeze*. An increase in the fertility rate over time, or a decrease in the infant and child mortality rate for a number of years, affects the marriage market. These changes result in greater numbers of people being born and surviving in each successive year, a process that diminishes the number of eligible partners at the time of marriage for each successive cohort. This situation is called a marriage squeeze, and it is described as follows. Brides typically choose mates from among a pool of men who are older than themselves. An increasing proportion of marriageable females in each year means there are proportionally fewer eligible older males to select from. Thus there are increasing numbers of women who might never marry. Conversely, if fertility rates decrease over consecutive years, or infant/child mortality increases, resulting in subsequently smaller birth cohorts, a marriage squeeze is experienced by men, since men marry women several years younger than themselves. So long as the preferred age difference between brides and grooms is fixed or rigid, fertility and mortality rates have a potentially powerful impact on the marriage market. On the other hand, if brides and grooms prefer and select mates of the same age, no marriage squeeze exists.

In the past the marriage market was a positive environment, enhancing a widow or widower's chances of marrying, if (a) a given society had flexible norms regarding the desired age spread between spouses; (b) marriage regulation permitted persons of different ages and social statuses to marry, or (c) the sex ratio was balanced.

We have reported the behaviors and attitudes associated with remarriage across a number of centuries for several countries in England and Europe. It is important to understand that there were a variety of practices related to remarriage that prevailed in regions other than western Europe. The next section provides some examples of remarriage customs in Asia.

REMARRIAGE IN ASIA

India

Almost every society has permitted the remarriage of a person when a first marriage ended, whether by death or divorce. One historical exception was medieval India. Dallas Fernando (1981) reports that between 500 and 1600 A.D. widows were not permitted to remarry, and this ban was enforced even when young girls were widowed in childhood. It was feared that the widow would conduct herself in such a way that would jeopardize the spiritual welfare of her dead husband. Since the widow was a member of the dead man's household, she was carefully watched and strongly censured if she misbehaved. Without a spouse to protect her from ill treatment in a family that was not her own, the well-being of a young widow was often in question. Her life could be quite miserable and held few joys. For example, she was not allowed to participate in any of the Hindu festivals because her presence was considered bad luck to everyone but her own children, if she happened to have any. Whether coerced by their dead husband's family members, or because of their own volition, many Hindu widows threw themselves on the funeral pyre of their dead spouse thus ending their own lives.

China

In premodern China in the city of Foochow, a widow could remarry. When she did, however, custom did not permit her to ride in the traditional red chair en route from her home to the home of her husband. The color of the widow's chair was black. Typically, Chinese culture fostered the same kind of conjugal devotion as thrived in India. Official policy toward the remarriage of widows was generally one of disapproval, and conjugal devotion to the dead spouse was encouraged. Remarriage was less common among the wealthy than among the poor. Arthur Wolf

(1981) writes that it was not unusual for poor parents-in-law of a widow to compel the woman to remarry so they would not have to continue to support her.

Sri Lanka

An interesting account of remarriage in Sri Lanka (formerly Ceylon) comes from an Englishman, Robert Knox (1966). Knox was captured and held hostage for 19 years in the Kandyan Kingdom during the middle of the seventeenth century. He escaped in 1678 and wrote an account of the social customs he observed.

Knox wrote that in the Kandyan Kingdom divorce was common, and agreed to by common consent of the couple. Both men and women might be married four or five times before they settled into a relatively permanent union. However, even the seemingly final marriage could be dissolved. Extramarital sexual unions were common and were seldom grounds for divorce. However, there were strong sanctions against a married woman having sexual relations with a man of a lower caste. A man, on the other hand, could have sexual relations with a woman of a lower caste as long as he did not eat with her, or bring her home as a wife. If a couple agreed to divorce, a woman would usually return to her village and be cared for by her parents or her brothers. This was necessary because women usually did not inherit land, nor was there a custom of joint ownership of land between spouses. The wife's dowry was returned to her after divorce, along with any gifts (clothing, ornaments, and so on) that had been given to her during the marriage. These possessions made it easier for a divorced woman to contract a remarriage (Fernando, 1981).

Arabia

In pre-Islamic Arabia it was the woman or her proxy who chose and contracted with the groom, rather than the other way around. Divorced or widowed women made the approach themselves and selected their own second or subsequent husbands. During the very early years of Islam, this practice was continued. Men had the right to get a divorce, but a woman could petition a judge or ruler and be granted a divorce if she could make a case, or if her husband took a second wife without her knowledge and permission. Remarriage was permitted, and often had fewer restrictions than a first marriage.

In pre-Islamic Arabia there was no limit on the number of wives a man could take, and marriage, remarriage, polygyny and divorce were not clearly differentiated. This changed when polygyny was controlled by the introduction of Islam. The laws of Islam introduced the rule that a man should take only one wife—two or more would be the exception. Divorce was made costly, and material penalties were designed to make a man think long and hard before divorcing. According to Islamic rule, "amongst those acts which are permitted, divorce is the most detestable to Allah" (Huzayyin, 1981: 97).

REMARRIAGE IN THE UNITED STATES

Seventeenth Through Eighteenth Century

In colonial America, as in Europe during the same time period, remarriage following the death of a spouse was socially approved. It was a relatively common occurrence. However, death and remarriage rates varied from colony to colony. In New England, the living conditions were generally healthier than those in the South, and thus the death rate in New England was lower. When death did occur, remarriage quickly followed, usually within the first year and sometimes within six months. The Puritans felt it was wise for widows to marry rapidly in order to avoid idolizing their departed spouses. However, the interval between marriages did vary between the colonies. In Pennsylvania a 1690 law required that a widow wait at least a year before remarrying. The Quakers in New England also required both widows and widowers to wait a year before remarring.

We do not know for sure the typical number of remarriages that occurred among the early settlers. Arthur Calhoun (1917) wrote that second and even third marriages were common among the early New Netherlanders. In Massachusetts, however, fewer remarriages are recorded. In Plymouth Colony, 40% of the men and 25% of the women remarried once, while 6% of men and 1% of women remarried more than twice (Demos, 1970).

Over time, changes in the sex ratio influenced the remarriage rate in New England. By the third generation, the ratio of males to females had shifted due to female emigration and new births. This change affected the remarriage rate. In the first ten years of the eighteenth century only 10% of the women and 25% to 33% of the men in Woburn,

Massachusetts, remarried. Marcia Guttentag and Paul Secord (1983) report that the adult sex ratio was 87.9 in Woburn by 1765. Thus by the late eighteenth century there was an imbalanced sex ratio throughout New England in favor of men. This imbalance served to depress the chances of remarriage for women.

A study of remarriage in Newburyport, Massachusetts, by Susan Grigg (1977) illustrates how sex, age, the presence of children, and economic well-being affected remarriage probabilities in New England. Her findings show that half of the widowers eventually remarried compared to only 20% of the widows, and widowers remarried much more quickly. The average duration of widowhood for men was 1.9 years; for widows it was 5.6 years. Remarriage was closely associated with age. Records show that remarriage was most likely to occur for both men and women under the age of 30, and it did not occur at all for the oldest 18% of either men or women. For widowers, the presence of children aged 5 to 15 reduced the likelihood of remarriage, whereas the presence of older and younger children increased it. Remarriage for widows was not associated with age of children. This study also showed that there was no association between a husband's wealth at the time of his wife's death and the likelihood of his remarriage. For widows, however, wealth was confounded with age. Widows with the highest and lowest valuation were relatively old and their remarriage rates were correspondingly low. Another study that examined remarriage in Salem, Massachusetts, in 1800 also documented an inverse relation between wealth and remarriage for women (Farber, 1972).

In the South the situation was somewhat different than in New England. Health hazards made life more problematic there, for malaria, dysentery, and influenza caused many deaths. Life was fragile for both men and women. Even so, women tended to outlive their husbands. In Charles County, Maryland, for example, women outlived men by a ratio of two to one, and women took new husbands three times more often than men took new wives. Because the sex ratio favored women, many women married two or three times (Carr and Walsh, 1983). One historian reports that in Charles County marriage was likely to last only seven years, with only a 33% chance of lasting 10 years before one partner died (Walsh, 1977). Another study reporting on orphaned children claims that about 25% of the children in seventeenth-century Virginia had lost one or both parents by the age of 5; by the age of 13 over half had lost a parent, and 70% had experienced parental loss by the age of 21 (Fox and Quitt, 1980).

Nineteenth Through Twentieth Century

As the nation grew and health care improved, the mortality rate for both males and females declined. However, marriages were still vulnerable—as the mortality rate declined, the rate of divorce increased.

After the American War of Independence, but especially after the Civil War, the divorce rate began to increase. Divorce rather than death became the reason many marriages ended. However, it was not until 1973-1974 that the number of dissolutions due to divorce superceded those caused by death.

World War I influenced the marriage rate in this country dramatically. There was an upswing in the number of marriages entered into during the first months of the United State's involvement in the war. The increase continued during registration for service, and during the first months of military training. The rate declined, however, during the following year when many eligible young men were overseas. The postwar (1919-1920) remarriage rate for widowed persons was very high. Many husbands had died in the war, and many men and women had died in the American flu epidemic of 1918—these events left almost 200,000 relatively young persons widowed (Jacobson, 1959).

During the early 1930s, marriage, divorce, and remarriage rates declined. The decline in remarriages of divorced persons during the Great Depression likely resulted from the reduction in the number of divorce decrees that were sought. The depression also had an impact on the remarriage rate of widows. The poor economic conditions caused many to postpone marriage and thousands of widows lost their opportunity for marriage. A widow's chances for marriage are generally most favorable in the years immediately after her bereavement. For most women of middle age, delay in marriage for even a few years puts them at an age when the men they would have married pass them by to marry younger women (Jacobson, 1959).

The pattern during World War II was fairly similar to that of World War I. The marriage rate rose during the early years of the war, declined during its midcourse, increased immediately during the postwar years, and then reverted more or less to its prewar level (Jacobson, 1959).

After the surge in marriage and divorce rates following World War II had settled back to prewar levels, the general trend shows a slight decrease in the marriage rate for the first half of the 1950s. Then began a slow increase that peaked in 1972. Since 1972 the first-marriage rate has declined. On the other hand, the divorce rate decreased slightly during the early 1950s, and began a dramatic upward surge in the mid-1960s. Although there was a slight tapering off of the divorce rate about 1980, a moderate rise is expected by the end of the 1980s. Demographers currently estimate that in the mid-1980s about 50% of all first marriages will eventually end in divorce (Glick, 1984).

The remarriage rate follows a similar pattern. By the late 1960s the remarriage rate was only slightly above that of the postwar 1940s, whereas the divorce rate was far greater. The remarriage rate started to decline even before the mid-1970s while the divorce rate continued to rise (Carter and Glick, 1976).

There has been a good deal of speculation about the recent trends as demographers and family scholars try to explain the unpredicted leveling off of both marriage and remarriage rates and the rise in divorce. Cherlin (1981) summarizes the most widely accepted explanations. First, there was a greater tolerance of divorce beginning in the mid-1960s. The upsurge in divorce began in the early 1960s, and Cherlin suggests that a change in attitude came *after* the change in behavior. Second, there were more married women in the labor force. This was associated with greater job opportunities for women, which led to their greater economic independence. When women are not dependent on men for their economic well-being, they are more likely to leave an unhappy marriage and seek divorce. Similarly, men may also feel more freedom to leave marriages in which they are unhappy if they perceive their spouse is not economically dependent upon them. Third, there was a decline in the relative income of the large postwar male birth cohort, making it necessary for wives to enter the labor force if couples were to maintain their accustomed standard of living. We have already mentioned the effects of women's labor force participation. Finally, the introduction of contraception indirectly played a role. Effective contraception techniques permitted working wives to delay reproductive behavior. Since the presence of children serves to increase wives' dependence on their husbands, the absence of children facilitated marital dissolution (Morgan and Rindfus, 1985).

THE CURRENT PICTURE

The current remarriage rate in the United States closely parallels that of an earlier time in Europe and colonial America, at about 20%–30% (Griffith, 1980; Laslett, 1977). What has changed is the fact that remarriage follows divorce rather than death. As was true in an earlier era, men currently remarry more often than women and do so more quickly after both divorce and bereavement. Age still influences the remarriage potential in the United States today. Generally the widowed are older than the divorced and hence are less likely to remarry. However, census data show that even men and women in early middle age are more likely to remarry if their marriages end in divorce rather than the death of their spouse. When the widowed do remarry, the median age for widowers is about 60 (as of 1978) and for widows the comparable age is 53. In 1978 the median age at remarriage for divorced men was 36 and for women it was 30.

The median interval between first marriage and divorce is about seven years, and the median interval between divorce and remarriage is three years (Spanier and Glick, 1981). Also, there is an equal tendency for a divorced person to choose a mate who has never been married as one who has been married before. A 1985 study showed that among the 9.2 remarried (after divorce) households in the United States, 30% of them consisted of a divorced woman and a first-married man, 35% consisted of a divorced man and a first-married women, and in 35% of the households both spouses had been divorced (Cherlin and McCarthy, 1985).

Social class differentially affects remarriage for men and women. Among divorced persons, education and income levels are negatively associated with remarriage for women and positively associated with remarriage for men. That is, women in lower classes remarry more often than women in higher classes. For men, the opposite is true: Higher-educated men with higher income levels remarry more quickly.

Remarriage rates also vary by race. Although the first-marriage rate is higher among whites than blacks, the separation and divorce rate is higher for blacks. However, the redivorce rate for whites is higher than for blacks.

CONCLUSION

This chapter described the remarried situation at many different times and places around the world. One primary fact separates the past situation from the current one. That is, although remarriage was a common practice among our European ancestors, it generally followed the death of a spouse. Remarriage in the United States today usually follows divorce. Demographers now estimate that almost half of all first marriages begun in 1980 will end in divorce. The corresponding figure for second or subsequent marriages is about 60%. Thus the evidence is clear that remarriages are more vulnerable to dissolution then are first ones. Why this is true is not entirely clear, although there has been some speculation. In the chapters that follow we try to explain why the development of marital relationships and adjustment to stepfamily life are so difficult.

DISCUSSION QUESTIONS

(1) Why do you think attitudes toward remarriage changed over time during the Middle Ages?
(2) What is the marriage market? List the factors that influence it.
(3) Explain the continued rise in the divorce rate and the decrease in the marriage rate in the United States in terms of historical events. How are age, the sex ratio, social class, and race related to probabilities of remarriage?
(4) How might remarriages following death differ from those following divorce?

RELATED READINGS

CHERLIN, A. (1981) Marriage, Divorce, Remarriage. Cambridge, MA: Harvard University Press.

DUPAQUIER, J., E. HELIN, P. LASLETT, M. LIVI-BACCI, and S. SOGNER (1981) Marriage and Remarriage in Populations of the Past. New York: Academic Press.

LEVITAN, S. A. and R. BELOUS (1981) What's Happening to the American Family? Baltimore, MD: Johns Hopkins University Press.

CHAPTER
3

Family Structure and Family Process

Step   [ME. < OE. steop-, orphaned (akin to G. stief-, ON.
                stjup-) < base of stiepan, to bereave, prob < IE.
                (s)teub-, to strike (hence "cut off"), whence STUMP,
                STEEP; orig. used of orphaned children] a combining
                form meaning related through the remarriage of a
                parent [stepchild, stepparent]

Blend   [ME. blenden, OE. blendan & ON. blanda, to mix
                IE. base bhlendh-, to glimmer indistinctly, whence
                BLIND, BLUNDER] 1. To mix or mingle,. . . espe-
                cially so as to produce a desired flavor, color, grade,
                etc. 2. To mix or fuse thoroughly, so that the parts
                merge and are no longer distinct.

Reconstitute   To constitute again or renew; reconstruct, reorganize,
                or recompose; specif., to restore. . .
                                    —Webster's New World Dictionary

THE DEFINITION OF "step" as quoted here reflects the point we made
in Chapter 2 about death being the *raison d'etre* for remarriage in earlier
times. The definitions of the second and third terms reflect modern
usages designed to convey meaning about contemporary stepfamilies.
Blended and *reconstituted* are the two most frequently used labels for
remarried families. Both of the latter terms suggest that the stepfamily
is made up of disparate parts that are joined together to make one unit.
These separate parts and the processes involved in making them "one"
is the subject of this chapter.

In the pages that follow we analyze the different components of family
structure (the parts) and the processes associated with maintaining that
structure. Specifically, we examine the processes of commitment, cohesion, communication, and boundary maintenance—processes that
operate in all families.

Because structure is central to this discussion, we devote several pages
to a clarification of the concept. Then we distinguish between different
"types" of remarried family structures reported in the literature. Finally,
we examine the ways that the processes of commitment, cohesion, communication, and boundary maintenance may operate differently in
remarriage than in first marriage.

FAMILY STRUCTURE

The *structure* of any unit—whether a microscopic cell, a large
bureaucratic organization, or a family—is the arrangement of the unit's

interdependent parts to create a definite pattern of organization. When we speak of the structure of a family we are talking about the inter-dependent parts—all the members of that family, including kin that may reside outside the family's boundary. We are also talking about the way the family is organized, or ways that family members interact with one another in their daily activities. Several important components of organization are presented in the following section. For some of you this discussion will be a review. For others it will be an introduction to salient sociological concepts related to family organization.

An essential element of family organization is its *division of labor*— the allocation of responsibilities, duties, and tasks among family members: Who in the family does what to get the family work accomplished? The division of labor can take several different forms. For example, domestic labor can be distributed according to traditional sex roles, with female members doing the housework and male members doing the repair, maintenance, and outside work. Or family work can be distributed according to skill, interest of members, or who has the time at any particular moment. Allocation of work also is based upon some principle of justice. That is, work can be assigned on the basis of equality (equal share) or equity (fair or proportional share).

A second component of organization is the rules, or *norms* that guide the behavior of family members. Norms are the standards of behavior that govern family interactions. They are determined in part by the larger culture, but they also develop within individual families. Thus norms may vary from family to family in any community. For example, in one family all members may be expected to show up at dinnertime, because it is the designated time for members to come together to talk and share information about each individual's daily activities or topics of interest. Compare this to the norms of another family, where the eating activity is valued in and of itself, where dinnertime is simply the designated time to consume food. Family rules concern minor issues as well as major ones. For example, is it inappropriate to bounce a ball in the house, leave the cap off the toothpaste, or forget to put the toilet seat down after use?

Many factors shape the norms that family members adopt. Religious values, racial or ethnic identity, and social status help determine the norms that are established within any family. Personal habits and preferences also determine the rules a family adopts.

Norms are usually accompanied by some set of *sanctions* (rewards and punishments) that are used to reinforce adherence on the part of family members. Sanctions can be as subtle as the laugh from a parent when a child tells a joke, or as obvious as spanking a child for misbehavior or depriving a teenager of the use of the family car.

A third component of family social organization is the assignment of *roles* that family members play, or roles that members assume for themselves. Roles are the expected behaviors associated with family positions of mother, son, sister, and so on. Roles associated with the "mother" position include, among a host of others, nurturer, discipliner, counselor, and nurse. Roles can also have psychological dimensions, as when siblings compete for their own place or identity within the family. The "mother's helper" role is often secured by the oldest daughter and is associated with personality dimensions such as dependability and responsibility. When the "helper" role is taken, a second daughter may assume another role, such as the family "slob," "comedian," or "athlete" in order to find a unique place in the family that establishes her special identity.

Family positions and roles have attached to them different degrees of *power*. It is the norm in well-functioning families for parents to be the authority figures and to hold the highest status, and thus to hold the most power. In cultures where three-generation families share the same household, higher status may reside with the oldest generation. However, in most nuclear families in the United States, parents hold the most power. When parental power is abdicated in the family, family functioning is impaired and can result in maladaptive or destructive child behaviors (Olson et al., 1979; Peek et al., 1985).

Now consider the units that make up the family structure. The traditional American family is a *nuclear* family, that is, a family made up of an adult couple or a single parent and the biological or adopted minor child(ren) of that couple/parent. Although the American family household typically holds only two generations, some households do have three generations, for example, an older, grandparent generation may live with their married child and grandchildren, a young teenage mother with her child may live with the mother's parents, a young married couple and their children may live with grandparents, or a divorced, single parent may return to his or her family of origin with his or her children. *Extended kin* are relatives other than parents and their child(ren) of the immediate family, including aunts, uncles, grandparents, and cousins. Some relatives are considered more important than others in the American kinship system. In-laws, grandparents, adult siblings, as well as second- and third-level cousins are often counted as members of the family. *Quasi kin* is a concept introduced into the vocabulary of family scholars by Paul Bohannan (1970). Quasi kin refers to a formerly married persons's ex-spouse, the ex-spouse's new husband or wife, and his or her blood kin. These people are part of the extended kin network of remarried persons. Chapter 6 will discuss in detail how remarriage can affect and sometimes complicate involvement with extended kin.

THE EFFECT OF DIVORCE AND REMARRIAGE ON FAMILY STRUCTURE

When a marriage ends in divorce, the two spouses typically separate and set up two households where before there was only one—ignoring for the moment the spouse who returns to his or her parental home to live. According to sociologist Jessie Bernard (1980: 568), 14.4% of divorced women in the mid-1970s went "home to mother" after divorce. Although the public image may be that ex-spouses terminate all aspects of their relationship, in reality what little data there is on this topic show a high degree of contact between former spouses after divorce. One study found that one year after divorce 48% of divorced couples reported talking with each other about the former marriage and 36% talked about why they had divorced; 44% talked about personal problems (Goldsmith, 1980). If the divorcing adults have no children, there is likely to be less contact between them (Bloom and Kindle, 1985). If the couple have a child and both want to continue parenting roles, it is difficult to discontinue contact. In that case, the two ex-partners and the households they establish are joined both legally and emotionally, though not physically, by the existence of the child.

If and when the former spouses remarry (we learned in Chapter 2 that most of them do), the child's kin network expands; stepparents, stepgrandparents, stepsiblings, and half-siblings may join the family. Along with the parents, this expansion creates what Jacobson (1982) has termed the *linked family system.* Figure 1 illustrates Jacobson's conceptualization of the linked households, a family situation for which Constance Ahrons (1979) coined the term *binuclear family.* According to Ahrons, a binuclear family is "a family style that does not force the child to sever the bond with either parent and which allows both parents to continue to enact their parental roles postdivorce" (p. 499).

The situation is different for marriages that end because one spouse dies. When death ends a marriage, the binuclear family or linked family

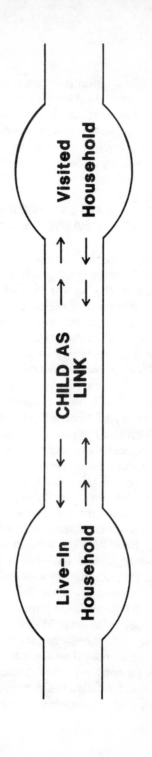

Figure 1: Jacobson's Conceptualization of the Linked Family System
SOURCE: Jacobson (1982).

system cannot exist, although there may continue to be contact with the family of the deceased spouse. Thus some of the complexities associated with remarriage are eliminated when remarriage follows bereavement. This does not imply that remarriage following widowhood is not subject to many of the same problems as remarriage following divorce. Widowed persons who become stepparents face many of the same situations as the divorced who become stepparents, and relations with extended kin may be just as complicated.

It is chiefly the complexity of family structure that differentiates remarried from first-married families. Membership in the binuclear family includes the addition of new members plus the often complicated interpersonal relationships between "old" and "new" members. The child, as a member of a binuclear family, has two sets of authority figures, two sets of rules in two homes, and two different hierarchies of status and prestige—all this makes the remarried family more complex. When a marriage breaks up, there has to be a change in the division of labor in the household. If children are in the family, the parent who continues to live with and care for the children also assumes responsibility for all the household tasks that were formerly shared by two adults. Remarriage brings with it the potential for a new sharing or division of household labor. However, with the new partner may come different expectations about the way to do things, and dissimilar standards as to how much "help" the children should or should not contribute. In addition, the presence of stepsiblings and/or half-siblings can influence the children's status hierarchy differently in the two families. A last-born child in one family may suddenly find himself or herself "in the middle" in a remarried family. The favored "baby" position is no longer his or hers. Rewards and punishments may differ between the two homes, as can role allocations and role expectations. Keeping track of where everything goes in two homes, or keeping track of his or her own possessions, can be frustrating for some children. One 11-year-old boy who had for several years spent half the week in one household and half in the other got his two sets of parents together and negotiated for change. He said, "I want to have all my underwear in one drawer!" How children cope with this complexity has been the subject of much speculation. Finally, a not irrelevant factor in the establishment of binuclear families is the nature of the relationship between the adults in the two homes. That is, is it characterized by positive, negative, or neutral affect?

To summarize, within any family unit there will be persons who fill positions. These positions will be hierarchically arranged; hence some persons will have more power than others. There will be some system whereby domestic tasks are allocated and there will be sets of rules or norms established that specify the roles attached to each position. There will be toleration limits established as to what is viewed as acceptable behavior. When conforming behavior is enacted, positive sanctions reward family members. Nonconformity is interpreted as deviance, and punished with negative sanctions. The totality of all the individuals in the family, nuclear and extended, plus the pattern of organization make up the family structure. Family structure increases in complexity after divorce and remarriage. With the establishment of two households, a child's world has the potential of expanding and including four parents and innumerable extended kin. In the best of all possible worlds this means that children in remarriages have the benefit of double love, resources, and assistance. Whether or not this potential is realized depends on the amount of contact the adults in both households maintain with the child(ren), and the quality of that contact. It also is dependent upon the kinds of feelings that are associated with the contact adults have with each other. A system may evolve that permits child(ren) to move freely and regularly between two homes. This may or may not cause stress, depending on the nature of the relationship between adults.

Family scholars have attempted to describe the types of structure that emerge as a result of remarriage. Several of these efforts are described in the next section.

TYPOLOGIES OF FAMILY STRUCTURE

The creation of typologies is a first step in theory building. Typologies help to describe and summarize the breadth and range of phenomenon. Scholars have conceptualized and classified types of remarriage according to a variety of different characteristics of the remarried couple/individual. Each of these types conceptualizes remarriage in a slightly different way. Demographers tend to be interested only in the marital status of the remarrying couple, categorizing remarriages on that basis. For example, Sogner and Dupaquier (1981) are European demographers who distinguish between three types of remarriage using rather dated terms. They categorize remarriages contracted between (a) widowers and spinsters, (b) widows and bachelors, and (c) widowers and widows. Their typology expands to eight distinct groups for societies that permit divorce, that is, a divorced man and a spinster, a divorced man and a widow, and a divorced man and a divorced woman, and so on.

A second classification system is based upon the presence of children, inferring the residential status of children. According to Benjamin Schlesinger (1970) remarriages may involve (a) a father, his own child, and a new mother (stepmother families); (b) a mother, her own child, and a new father (stepfather families); and (c) a father, his own child, plus a mother and her own child (stepfather/stepmother families). This classification expands further if one includes children born to the new remarriage (called "joint" or "child in common"): joint child/stepmother, joint child/stepfather, and joint child/stepmother/stepfather families. Schlesinger's system refers only to stepfamilies and leaves out the remarried couple who have no children.

Ahrons (1980) developed a typology for classifying binuclear family structures. This classification scheme hints at the complexity of relationships that develop between two households when adults parent the same child(ren). The least complex of these is the situation (a) where neither former spouse has a new partner—that is, no remarriage has taken place. A situation (b) where only one former spouse has a new partner is the next most complex, followed by the most complex family structure (c) where both former spouses each have a new partner. Because Ahrons was interested in cooperative parenting and distinguishing between different coparenting relationships, several subtypes were developed from the three primary types listed. These include remarried households where mother has custody, father has custody, parents share joint custody, or parents have split custody.

Sociologist Jean Giles-Sims (1984b) also utilized the binuclear family as the basis for developing her typology, incorporating two new elements: feelings of affect and degree of contact between members of the two households. Her fourfold typology includes the following:

(1) *Interdependent-positive families.* These are families with a high degree of contact and positive feelings expressed by family members toward members of the "other" household.
(2) *Interdependent-negative families.* These families experience a high degree of contact but it is accompanied by negative feelings toward those in the "other" household.
(3) *Independent-positive families.* The members of the two households have little contact with each other and the "positive" affect actually represents a tolerance or relief for the lack of contact and involvement between families.

(4) *Independent-negative families.* These families also are characterized by lack of contact and noninvolvement between the binuclear households, but in this case feelings of resentment and hostility accompany the lack of contact.

Therapist Margaret Robinson (1980) devised a threefold classification of stepfamilies based upon the marital status of the biological parent: (a) a legitimating stepfamily—one where a man or woman (usually a man) marries a never-married parent with a child; (b) a revitalized stepfamily—one where a man or woman marries a widow or widower with a child; and (c) a reassembled stepfamily—one where a man or woman marries a divorced parent with a child.

Finally, one last classification scheme is reviewed—the ninefold typology of family structure that we developed (Pasley and Ihinger-Tallman, 1980). This scheme does not consider the relationship between two households, as Ahron's and Giles-Sims's do. Rather, it was developed in an attempt to emphasize the degree of complexity present in a remarried family. Three characteristics (the presence or absence of children, the relationship of those children to the remarried husband and wife, and the residence of children) serve as the basis for this classification. Each type represents an increasing level of family complexity:

(1) Remarried spouses, both of whom are childless. This type of family is not structurally different from a first-married one except that at least one spouse has prior marital experience.

(2) Remarried spouses who only have a child with the current partner—a child-in-common. Again, this type resembles a first-married couple, except for the prior marital experience of at least one of the spouses. The fact of the parent's previous marriage(s) is irrelevant to the child of this union.

(3) Remarried spouses, at least one of whom has an adult child from a previous marriage. Here the differentiating factor is the adult status of the offspring. Remarriage is expected to be somewhat different for couples who are past the age of parenting minor children. This is not to say that older couples do not encounter difficulties pertaining to children. Rather, the issues and problems related to child rearing are not part of their daily lives.

(4) Remarried spouses who have a child in common and one or both partners have a child from a previous marriage who does not reside with the couple. The couple may or may not have the nonresidential child visit.

Here the remarried couple approximates a first family by having their own biological child. However the presence of a nonresidential child who occasionally visits his or her parent is a distinguishing characteristic of this remarriage type.

(5) Remarried spouses with no children in common, but at least one of the partners has a child from a previous marriage and the child does not reside with the couple. The nonresidential child may or may not visit. In this case the child is a potential participant in the couple's life but usually only on a visiting basis. Frequency of visits may vary widely, from regular weekly visits to extremely rare ones. However, custody arrangements do change, and remarried couples of this type could very well fall into category 6 at some point in time.

(6) Remarried spouses, at least one of whom has a child from a previous marriage residing in the home. This remarried type is labeled "simple," meaning children of only one spouse reside with the remarried couple.

(7) Remarried spouses, both of whom have a child from a prior marriage, residing in the home. This family incorporates stepsiblings as an aspect of its structure. This type is labeled "complex," meaning children of both spouses reside with the remarried couple. The following two types are variations of the complex stepfamily.

(8) Remarried spouses, both of whom have a child from a previous marriage residing with them, plus a child in common. The distinguishing characteristic here is a half-sibling as a member of the sibling group.

(9) Remarried spouses, both of whom have a child residing with them, plus a child in common, plus a nonresidential child of one or both spouses living elsewhere. This type of stepfamily is the most complex of all, incorporating all possible contingencies. It includes stepmother, stepfather, stepsibling, and half-sibling positions, plus residential and nonresidential children. This typology helps us see the diversity of remarried families. There is no one kind of stepfamily.

In summary, several typologies were identified and summarized. Each accentuated different characteristics of remarried families: the marital status of the couple, the presence of children, the remarried couple's relationship to another household, and finally, the marital status of a parent combined with the degree of complexity observed in the living arrangements of adults and children.

The nature of interaction within the family, and between the family and the community, is influenced at least in part by the structure depicted in these typologies. For example, the physical presence of children surely complicates family interaction. As the number of children increase and their residence varies, interaction is further complicated. It is not only the frequency of contact that influences stepfamily life, but the emotional and psychological presence of children (even if they are not physically present) also affects couple interaction. Up to this point we have discussed structure. In order to understand another aspect of remarriage we next turn to a discussion of the processes that inhibit or enhance the development of successful family functioning.

FAMILY PROCESS

Social scientists have identified several important behaviors that must occur within small groups (such as the family) if the group is to function effectively. Four factors—commitment, cohesion, communication, and the maintenance of the group's boundaries—are identified by social psychologists as particularly important for the formation and stable maintenance of groups like the family (Tallman, 1976). Because these concepts represent behaviors that are abstract and subject to change, we refer to them as processes. The four processes identified can be particularly problematic in remarried families. For example, the process of developing commitment and cohesion among family members who may not like each other or may not want another member to be considered "in the family" clearly makes it more difficult to establish a cohesive unit. The development of effective communication between family members who might prefer not to communicate is a complicated process. And determining how open or closed the family should be to outside people and pressures is a formidable task. Each of these family processes is discussed next.

Commitment

The essence of commitment is the desire to maintain something (Leik and Leik, n.d.). Remarried couples must maintain their commitment to the marriage. At the same time they try to create an environment that fosters commitment to the family unit in other family members, especially children. Couples in first-married families are more likely to take for granted their children's family commitment simply because of the interdependency of members who grow and mature together. Although children's involvement in the family way decrease as they mature, they nevertheless suffer distress if their parents divorce, even when they are adults (Ihinger-Tallman, 1985). This type of automatic commitment to the family is rare among children in remarried families.

In some cases a high level of commitment may be missing even among remarrying adults. Two social workers, James Hunter and Nancy Schuman (1980), call attention to the low level of commitment they and their colleagues have observed on the part of some remarried parents toward maintaining a stable family unit. According to these professionals, the absence of commitment means that these remarried adults lack the motivation to make the sometimes painful adjustments and sacrifices that may be required to make the marriage work.

There are several reasons commitment to the remarriage may not stay high. Three quite different explanations have been proposed to explain the higher divorce rate among remarried couples than among first-married couples, that is, why remarried spouses do not remain committed to each other and to the marriage.

Terence Halliday (1980) offers a *selectivity* argument. He suggests that people who divorce and remarry are a select group of persons who are willing to end an unsatisfactory marriage. First marriages contain people who are more reluctant to divorce even though the quality of their marriages may also be poor. Thus this argument says that a lessened commitment and lack of motivation to solve marital problems stems from a predisposition of the participants rather than the quality of the marriage itself.

Recall Cherlin's (1978) *incomplete institution* hypothesis in Chapter 1. This hypothesis is the second reason offered to explain the higher divorce rate among remarrieds. Cherlin argues that the roles and norms associated with remarriage are poorly defined and unclear. This leads to behaviors that must be negotiated within each and every remarried family. When norms are not clear, behavior cannot be taken for granted, and people cannot fall back on "customary" behavior. For example, the way a stepmother chooses to behave toward a stepchild is not selected from a prescribed and understood "normative" set of behaviors. Rather, a stepmother must figure out for herself which role is most appropriate for her to enact: a distant acquaintance, a friend, a "best" friend, a parent, and so forth. If societal norms prescribed that stepmothers do not become emotionally close to their stepchildren for several years—if ever—every member of the remarried family would know what to expect. Then, whether or not a particular family's experience deviated from the norm would be determined by family members' behavior. But they would have a standard to measure their behavior against. As it is, many stepmothers believe that because they love the children's father, they will automatically love his children (called the myth of "instant love"). Many a shocked stepmother has confessed her discomfort in realizing and admitting that she does not feel love for her stepchildren. A weakened commitment to the remarriage on the part of both the step-mother and father might be the consequence of this perceived lack of affection. If the absence of love between stepmembers was accepted as normative, then shock, embarrassment, and guilt would be lessened among those who recognize and admit their lack of such feelings.

A third explanation for different commitment levels among remar-ried couples suggests that divorce and remarriage are *selective of unstable persons*—persons who have personal and emotional problems that make an enduring marriage difficult. Alcoholics, persons who are physically violent, or those who are emotionally unstable are likely to have mutliple marriages. Commitment of a partner may decrease as he or she realizes the unstable qualities of the spouse, and a decrease in commitment jeopardizes the marriage (Bergler, 1948; White and Booth, 1985).

Cohesion

Cohesion, or a sense of unity, is a quality of family life that characterizes how close family members feel to each other, whether they feel they belong to, and are proud of, their family (Giles-Sims, 1984b; Ihinger-Tallman and Pasley, 1981). When studying family cohesion, researchers measure the extent to which family members see themselves as loving, getting along well, and being uncritical of each other (Booth and Welch, 1978). A feeling of not belonging is less likely to be felt by family members in first marriages, although it can occur. Feelings of not belonging occur when the family is functioning poorly, as when one member is scapegoated or rejected. Or, sometimes a child or teenager may feel he or she doesn't fit into the family.

In remarried families cohesion is a characteristic that takes time and effort to develop. Some research (Asmundsson et al., 1983) reports that a time period of three to five years is necessary for cohesion to develop in remarried families. Family cohesion is created by behaviors such as finding each person a special "place" in the new family, estab-lishing cordial relationships with ex-spouses, and creating a new home that both parents and children feel comfortable calling theirs. Finally, in some cases the stress associated with solving problems can help to promote family cohesion. When annoyances are discussed and grievences aired the resolution of conflict promotes feelings of closeness and a sense of belonging (Asmundsson et al., 1983).

Communication

Harold Raush, Ann Greif, and Jane Nugent (1979) suggest that social class, age, sex, ethnic background, race, and cultural practices affect the nature of the communication among family members. In addition, personality and situational factors influence the style and content of communication. Raush and his colleagues also make the point that whatever influences one member's communication has repercussions throughout the family. A couple in a first marriage share a history wherein communication patterns develop simultaneously as the relationship evolves. Any children born into the marriage learn the family's style of communication as they grow. Thus although everybody misperceives and miscommunicates some of the time, there is likely to be less discrepancy between expectations and outcome for communication in first families than in stepfamilies. In first families, members come to know what to expect of one another, and they can interpret the remarks each makes within the context of family history. Siblings may say spiteful things to one another, but they are taught to believe that the other doesn't really mean it. Spouses know when their mate is annoyed or angry simply by the look on their face or the tone of voice. In other families, members do not express anger through argument, but through slammed cupboards and doors, and all family members know the signals.

When men and women begin a new marriage after divorce, they bring old communication habits to the new relationship. In one sense, this is not different from first marriages where two people must learn to interact with one another and establish clear patterns of communication. However, communication in the remarried family is more complex when children from a former marriage are part of the new family. In this situation, the negotiation process is confounded by unique or ideosyncratic habits and expections that were developed in two different families merged by the remarriage.

Several studies of remarried families indicate that the quality of communication between stepparent and stepchild is positively related to the family satisfaction of all members. Paul Koren and his colleagues (1983) report that children are more likely to feel satisfied and accepted when the communication with stepparent demonstrated affection and concern. Here, supportive communication between stepparent and stepchild was linked to the frequency of family activities as well as clear guidelines for behavior. In addition, supportive communication between husband and wife was negatively correlated with frequency of conflict and avoidance behavior. Thus the way remarried family members communicate their expectations of one another, their emotions, and their positive regard influences the overall satisfaction with membership in the family.

Boundary Maintenance

Family scholars agree that one of the most important tasks families must accomplish is defining and maintaining coherent boundaries around and within the family unit (Boss and Greenber, 1984; Walker and Messinger, 1979). Two boundaries in particular must be clearly defined: external boundaries and intergenerational boundaries. Remarried families have a third family boundary that must be defined and maintained: the interhousehold boundary that separates members of the binuclear household (Hunter and Schuman, 1980).

External boundaries represent the protective forces the family generates to "maintain their identity, security, and integrity against pressures from the outside world" (Tallman, 1976: 163). A secure external boundary insulates the family against undue interference from outside persons, such as social welfare workers, the police, or even friends.

How open or closed the boundaries are varies over time in any one family as well as between families. Family boundaries can be too open, permitting too many nonfamily persons access to the family, endangering the identity and integrity of the family unit. The opposite situation also may occur. Family boundaries can be too rigid or closed, isolating family members and preventing interaction with others in society. The ideal appears to be some middle ground of openness that protects the family, promotes healthy family functioning, and permits interaction between family members and the community.

Intergenerational boundaries are manifest in behavior that protects the identity, integrity, and security of the parental subsystem on one hand and the child-sibling subsystem on the other. A breakdown in intergenerational boundaries is evidenced by parent-child incest, stepparent-stepchild sexual intercourse, parental physical or psychological abuse of children, or teenage violence directed against parents. Less extreme behavior also jeopardizes the boundaries between the generations in a family. For example, when adults or children are not permitted the privacy accorded their position (sexual privacy for adults, the privacy of children's secrets recorded in a diary or letters), the integrity of the subsystem is endangered.

The violation of intergenerational boundaries also occurs when children are asked to assume roles that are inappropriate to their age. Some children assume the role of confidant to a single parent after separation, divorce, or during times of marital crisis. This adult role of "peer" is one that children are not always mature enough to handle. Similarly, when families are in crisis, an oldest child sometimes takes over the care of younger children in the household. Over time, role behavior that is inappropriate to the child's age may lead to adult-child role reversal, usually to the detriment of the child (Glenwick and Mowerey, 1986).

The *interhousehold boundary* is the third aspect of boundary establishment and maintenance relevant to binuclear households. When a divorced parent remarries, the interpersonal interactions with the former spouse, and sometimes with the children, are subject to change. This will be discussed in more detail in Chapter 6. Here we want to suggest the idea that the remarried couple may feel some pressure from others to make the boundaries around the new family more or less open than the couple might wish. There may be pressure from a spouse or an ex-spouse to permit nonresidential children to visit whenever they want. Conversely, the pressure may be to permit nonresidential children to visit less frequently or not at all. This situation occurs if there is hostility between the former spouses and resentment about the new marriage. Remarried families must accommodate children who do not live full time in the home and whose presence varies by the day of the week or season of the year (Whiteside, 1981). Boundaries must be open enough to permit this coming and going. An additional problem stems from the fact that all family members may not count those who come and go as family members. Family integrity is difficult to maintain when all members do not hold the same idea about who is in and who is out of the family. This problem exists for adults who are stepparents and children who are stepsiblings. One study of stepfamilies suggests that there may be some optimum level of openness of family boundaries. Where there is either too much or too little contact between binuclear family members then the marital quality of the remarried spouses decreases (Clingempeel, 1981).

Summary

Building relationships in remarried families is more difficult than in first families, especially when children are involved. This is because at least one of the spouses has prior marital experience, and the children in the family have learned the rules for appropriate behavior in another family context. Those rules may not be acceptable to the stepparent. When children are involved there are multiple sets of parents and siblings, as well as extended kin to integrate into the new family. Having family members who may or may not reside in the household and who hold emotional ties to another family makes it difficult to determine exactly who is in or out of the family. How family membership is determined varies within and between members in the binuclear unit. Such variation makes the establishment of family boundaries more difficult to achieve. When children serve as the link between two households, each family must help the children develop attachment and commitment to both units. To do this under conditions that include feelings of jealousy, rancor, indifference or hostility is obviously difficult. Similarly, even when there are no hostile feelings between households, turning each of the binuclear units into a cohesive, unified family is no easy task either.

Despite these difficulties, we remind the reader that many remarried families sucessfully negotiate the processes associated with commitment, cohesion, communication, and boundary maintenance. In spite of the difficulties, many remarried families make successful adaptations. In the next chapter we discuss the specific problems remarried couples face, and report the research that indicates the reasons for successful or failed negotiations.

DISCUSSION QUESTIONS

(1) Review the several components of family structure—division of labor, norms, sanctions, roles, and power. Provide examples, both positive and negative, of how these can affect remarriage *without* children compared to remarriages *with* children.

(2) How can typologies be used to help us understand stepfamily behavior?

(3) What other criteria could be used to develop new typologies of remarriage?
(4) What might members of remarried families do to foster commitment, cohesion, communication, and boundary maintenance?
(5) Which of the three reasons put forward to explain the higher divorce rate in remarriage do you think is the best? Why?

RELATED READINGS

TURNER, R. H. (1970) Family Interaction. New York: John Wiley.

WALD, E. (1981) The Remarried Family: Challenges and Promise. New York: Stepfamily Service Association of America.

CHAPTER
4

How Partners Adjust

(Wife, age 23, homemaker, married 1 year, 10 months): I feel anyone thinking about marrying a person who has been previously married should think very seriously about it. There are definitely special problems that accompany this type of marriage. I feel the couple should have counseling before and not marry until *all* doubts about the marriage are gone. I feel my husband and I will always have his previous marriage overshadowing our marriage. My husband also feels guilty for not having his children with him. I in turn feel guilty and feel if it wasn't for me, maybe my husband would get back with his ex-wife and kids and live happily ever after.

(Her husband, age 28, carpenter, married 1 year, 10 months): I think everyone should find the right spouse the first time. I found mine the second time and the only thing that stops it from being perfect is my previous marriage.

> —A Remarried Couple in
> Spokane, Washington

WHAT IS IT that makes a marriage satisfying? What makes it endure? In the previous chapter we noted that certain conditions associated with the development of commitment, cohesion, communication, and boundary maintenance foster the survival of a remarriage. In this chapter we explore whether cohabitation before remarriage influences couples' marital adjustment and satisfaction. We ask whether remarried couples report themselves to be any more or less satisfied with the quality of their marriage than first-married couples. We also take a look at some of the more frequently mentioned problems reported by remarried couples. We then examine boundary maintenance, loyalty conflicts, and resource distribution in more detail.

PREMARITAL COHABITATION

One question relevant to people interested in remarriage is whether cohabitation before marriage has positive or negative consequences for remarriage. Are divorced or widowed individuals who live together before they remarry any happier, better adjusted, or more satisfied in their marriage than individuals who do not cohabit?

Recent census figures indicate that in the United States about 4% of all couples are living together without being married to one another. This represents an increase of 300% from the number cohabiting in 1970 (Spanier, 1983). Of interest to us is that almost half of these cohabiting persons have previously been married: 47% of the men and 45% of the women are reported to be widowed or divorced.

Most of the research on the effects of unmarried cohabitation on the quality of marriage has included only first-married couples. A few studies do focus on remarried couples, or compare remarried and first-married couples. We review the findings from these studies next.

Is premarital cohabitation associated with greater marital satisfaction? Alfred DeMaris (1984) found marital satisfaction to be lower for husbands and wives in both first marriages and remarriages (N = 309 recently married couples) when they cohabited before marriage. However, the difference was statistically significant only for first-married couples. That is, cohabitation was negatively associated with marital satisfaction only for those couples who lived together before marrying for the first time. Sharon Hanna and Patricia Knaub (1981) studied 80 remarried couples, asking if cohabitation was a strengthening factor for remarriage. Their findings showed no differences between cohabitators and noncohabitators on the degree of marital satisfaction. Unpublished data from our own study (Pasley and Ihinger-Tallman, 1980) also found no significant relationship between cohabitation experience and marital satisfaction for 784 remarried husbands and wives.

The answer to our question, then, is no. The results of these few studies indicate that cohabitation with a future spouse is not associated with marital satisfaction among remarriers.

MARITAL SATISFACTION

Irrespective of cohabitation, studies that examine marital happiness or satisfaction have found only slight differences between first-married and remarried couples. Generally, the evidence suggests that remarried couples perceive their marriages to be only minimally less satisfying than couples who are in a first marriage. More important, significant sex differences are evident in many of the studies, with remarried husbands expressing more happiness or satisfaction than remarried wives. Karen Renne (1971) gathered a probability sample of 5373 respondents from one California county and found remarried people were somewhat more likely to be dissatisfied with their marriage than first-married people. Remarried wives reported more dissatisfaction than remarried husbands (with the exception of black remarried wives under age 45 who reported more satisfaction than black remarried husbands). Lynn White (1979) found no differences between remarried and first-married women and men, but did find significant sex differences. In her study first-married wives reported greater levels of global happiness (a slightly different measure of happiness than marital happiness) than did remarried women, whereas the opposite was true of first-married and remarried men. Norval Glenn and Charles Weaver (1977) found the 178 remarried women they studied reported lower levels of marital satisfaction than did the 196 remarried men. These data were gathered from three national surveys in the United States. A later study by Glenn (1981) analyzed National Opinion Research Center (NORC) data gathered during the years 1972 through 1978. He found remarried women reported less marital happiness than did first-married women. Remarried women also reported less happiness than their remarried male counterparts. Glenn found that responses from blacks were similar to whites, but the male-female differences were larger. Remarried black females reported more marital dissatisfaction than first-married black females, whereas black remarried males reported greater levels of marital satisfaction than first-married black males. Masako Ishii-Kuntz (1986) replicated Glenn's study with 1980 through 1985 NORC data. Her results were the same as Glenn's where sex differences were concerned. No differences in marital satisfaction were found, however, for first-marrieds versus remarrieds. Helen Weingarten (1980) found no differences in marital happiness between 184 remarried and 1068 first-married husbands and wives, after controlling for sex, education level, and length of marriage. In DeMaris's (1984) study on cohabitation reported earlier, he found no differences in marital satisfaction between the two groups irrespective of cohabitation experience. DeMaris did not find sex differences in reported marital satisfaction.

In summary, the findings from these studies are in agreement. Marital happiness levels appear to be about the same among first-married and remarried couples. Although slight differences were found in some studies, for the most part these differences are not statistically significant. Sex differences were found in six of the seven studies, with wives tending to report less satisfaction with their marriages than husbands.

A paradox is evident. If remarrieds report that they are as satisfied with their marriages as first-married couples are, why does the literature report multiple problems encountered by remarried couples? Also, what accounts for the slightly higher divorce rate among remarrieds? Are the problems associated with remarriage independent of feelings of satisfaction with marriage? Or are the couples who report satisfactory marriages those couples who have successfully solved the special problems of remarriage and hence have the most durable marriages? Have couples who are dissatisfied with their remarriage already divorced or separated early in the marriage, and thus removed themselves from the remarried population (and from the population of remarrieds available for study)? We will return to these issues later, after we report on the research that investigates the problems reported by remarried couples.

DIFFICULTIES IN MERGING TWO HOUSEHOLDS

Several studies have focused on identifying the problems in remarriage that may be associated with successful adjustment. Although there is some variation in the findings, an overall picture emerges that isolates some salient issues for a large number of remarried couples. We discuss this body of research next.

Problems Reported By Remarried Couples

Lillian Messinger (1976) found the two most frequent problems reported by 70 remarried couples were children and financial problems. These two problems appear in all other studies. For example, another study of 66 remarrieds found that the discipline of stepchildren, the stepparent being viewed as a "bad guy," problems with former spouses, and poor marital communication were the primary problems these couples faced (McClenahan, 1978).

Researchers Patricia Knaub, Sharon Hanna, and Nick Stinnett (1984) asked 80 remarried couples to identify the areas of conflict within their marital relationship. Responses revealed that discipline and the handling of children were considered to be the most problematic aspect of their marriage by over one-third of the respondents. A total of 32% of the couples rated financial difficulties as the source of most conflict, and 23% felt interpersonal concerns were the greatest source of conflict in their marriage. In all, 16% reported conflict associated with an ex-spouse, stepchildren, and noncustodial children.

In our own study (Ihinger-Tallman and Pasley, 1983) we asked 784 remarried persons how frequently they perceived disagreement in their marriage about 19 different topics we listed. It turned out that discipline of children and meeting children's needs were the most frequent sources of disagreement listed by both husbands and wives. The couple's inter-personal relationship itself was also a source of disagreement. Particular problem areas included quarrels over their sex life, not showing enough affection, and not having enough time alone together.

The Connecticut Remarriage Research Group (1983) studied 30 remarried families, including husbands, wives, and as many children as could be present at the time of interview. (Only responses from the adults were reported.) Fully half of these couples indicated that discipline and difficulties with adolescents were problems. Not having enough time together or for socializing with friends, financial problems that were unassociated with alimony or child support, and strain within the marital relationship itself were also mentioned.

From the stepchild's perspective, Patricia Lutz (1983) questioned 103 teenagers, all living in stepfamilies, about the issues that caused the most stress in their lives. Although none of the topics she asked about were highly stressful, two areas that teens felt to be somewhat stressful were loyalty conflicts and discipline from a stepparent—specifically, new rules, accepting discipline from a stepparent, and dealing with a stepparent's expectations.

Koren and his colleagues in Oregon (1983) interviewed a sample of 66 remarried families at three different points in time over an 18-month period. Early on (after about four months of living together), the two problems that were viewed as major were insufficient time to be alone and interference from ex-spouses and relatives. The same question was asked of the 47 families remaining in the study 18 months later. For both spouses the incidence of the most common problems did not change, although new problems were reported. About two years into the marriage husbands reported that four behaviors were more prob-lematic than earlier in the marriage. These included family members teaming up against each other, parents not supporting one another in parenting, one parent needing to "referee" child-parent disputes, and one parent withdrawing from the family. Thus, not only did the old prob-lems remain unsolved but new ones arose over time.

The children in this study (ages 9 to 18) were asked the same ques-tions about the family problems but the children's responses were slightly different from their parents'. In the first few months of the marriage children felt that money and finances, home manners and social habits, insufficient money, and lack of respect for privacy and personal space were the primary problems causing disagreements. The children listed "lack of respect for privacy" and "criticism of the nonresidential parent" as the two most severe problems at the end of the study 18 months later. By the end of the study one new problem was cited by children: insufficient time for parents to be alone together. The authors suggest that by a year and a half into the marriage, children were more sensitive to "the importance of marital accord to their parents' happiness" (Koren et al., 1983: 74). Overall, the incidence of problems cited by the adults and children in this study increased over time, and some early problems persisted. However, they did not necessarily increase in severity. Other researchers also make this observation, that less positive evaluations of family life do not seem to change over time (Pink and Wampler, 1985; Furstenberg, forthcoming).

The nature of discipline problems varies with each particular family, depending on the age of the children. However, the following quote from a 32-year-old homemaker, remarried 4 years, eloquently describes a common source of the problem:

> The only comment I would like to make is regarding the problem that is hard to overcome in my remarriage, which concerns the children. I will state that I feel my present marriage is good and far better than the first, but this one obstacle does create hard feelings and sometimes bitterness between myself and my spouse.
>
> Sometimes I feel he is too harsh in disciplining, or he doesn't have the patience to explain why he is punishing and to carry through in a calm manner, which causes me to have to step into the matter (which I probably shouldn't do). I also feel he could show more open affection to the children. I do realize that it was probably hard for my husband to enter marriage and the responsibility of a family instantly and I do give him a lot of credit for that. But this has remained a problem.

Clearly, parent-child relationships are problematic for members of stepfamilies. From clinicians we gather insights to more specific issues, particularly in the area of stepparent-stepchild relations. For example, David Mills (1984) suggests that one of the complications in stepparenting is that the biological parent (usually the mother) tends to interfere when the new spouse attempts to set limits for the child. This can be done in overt ways, such as when the mother verbally chastises the stepfather in front of the child for what she believes is inappropriate parenting behavior. More often, it is done in a covert manner. For example, a stepfather disciplines the stepchild who responds with, "That's not fair." The child then goes to his or her mother to complain about the stepfather's behavior and the mother communicates to the child that she'll take care of it, implying that the stepfather was wrong. She thus effectively undermines his status in the new family. Over time he begins to feel disenfranchised and an outsider to the rest of the family.

In summary, the attempt to discover the particular problems faced by remarried couples consistently identifies three distinct problem areas. Namely, children (particularly the discipline of children), money and finances, and the couple's interpersonal relationship. More important, problems that surface early in the marriage apparently persist.

Boundary Maintenance

In earlier chapters we mentioned that establishing and maintaining family boundaries is problematic for many remarried couples. This problem is often mentioned by clinicians who counsel remarrieds. Do remarrieds who are not seeking help for some problem also report they have trouble establishing the boundaries of the family unit and protecting the identity of their family? Few have studied this issue.

One difficulty in studying this problem is getting a good measure of boundary maintenance. The problem has been resolved by some researchers who asked family members to name the persons they considered to be in their family. When a family member such as a biological parent, a stepparent, or a stepchild who lives in the same household is left off such a list, this omission is taken as an indicator of unclear boundaries. A study designed by Frank Furstenberg, Nicholas Zill, and James Peterson (Furstenberg et al., 1983) involved telephone interviews with a sample of 1377 children and one of each child's parents. This study provides important insights into the extent of boundary ambiguity among the families of the children whose parents divorce and remarry. When asked "Who do you include in your family?" 15% of stepparents failed to include a stepchild in their list, even when the stepchild lived in the household, whereas only 1% of parents failed to list their own biological children. Children, too, left the names of parents and stepparents off their list. A total of 7% of the children excluded a biological mother, 9% excluded a biological father, and 31% did not mention a residential stepmother or stepfather as part of their family. When these researchers examined the data to see if there was greater boundary clarity among stepfamilies of longer duration, the results did not change. Thus "time alone does not guarantee that family boundaries will be redrawn" (Furstenberg, forthcoming: 13).

Our remarriage study (Pasley and Ihinger-Tallman, 1980) also included several questions that were designed to measure boundary ambiguity. One question asked, "Who's in your family?" Overall, 39% of the couples displayed some type of boundary ambiguity; 18% did not share the same perceptions about who was in the family, nor did they list the same family members as residing in the household; 13% indicated similar household membership (who lives in your home), but did not list the same people as members of the family; and 8% agreed on who was in the family, but failed to list the same people as residing in the household (Pasley, forthcoming). In addition, we were able to determine which member of the family was the most commonly omitted. As might be expected, we learned that the nonresidential child was the forgotten member. Typically, this omission occurred in stepmother families or in families where both adults were stepparents.

Clearly, these findings suggest a lack of clarity regarding membership in stepfamilies. Not only do children fail to include stepparents but adult stepfamily members also fail to include children—particularly children who are stepchildren and live elsewhere are excluded.

Another way boundary ambiguity has been measured is by examining the permeability of the family boundary. Glenn Clingempeel (1981) examined the relation between marital quality and frequency of contact with quasi kin (his measure of permeability). He found that marital quality was highest in stepfamilies that had moderate contact with the "other" family.

In another examination of boundary maintenance we (Ihinger-Tallman and Pasley, 1981) hypothesized that the more permeable the family boundary, the lower the marital stability of the spouses. This time we measured permeability in several ways: the frequency with which other people visited the couple's home, the frequency of contact with helping agencies and other community organizations, and the degree to which spouses shared their troubles with others (friends, relatives, counselors, and clergy). Results showed differences for husbands and wives on these measures. For husbands, visitation positively contributed to marital stability and contact with helping agencies decreased it. These two factors were also contributors for wives in the same way as for their husbands. An interesting finding resulted when we examined "sharing troubles." If wives shared their problems with others, this sharing was associated with less stability. Perhaps when there were a lot of troubles to share the marriage was in trouble anyway. However, if wives perceived that their husbands shared problems with others, this perception was associated with greater stability. We suggested that since the more stable families' boundaries were generally open to a wide array of others (measured by home visits), then the opportunity to share was present. Wives therefore might have generalized that if the opportunity was there, then men would take advantage of it. Or perhaps they perceived openness and good communication between themselves and their husbands and they generalized this openness to sharing with others outside the family. In point of fact, there were no differences in actual sharing of troubles between the men in stable and unstable marriages, but the perception of wives was strong enough to influence their own (wives') level of stability.

In summary, research findings suggest that there is a great deal of boundary ambiguity in remarriage. Studies show it is not uncommon for members of remarried families to forget to mention the names of immediate family members when asked about who is in their family. This omission is indicative of ambiguous family boundaries and is taken as indicating a weak sense of family identity. Attempts to measure boundary permeability have been few. Our own study suggested permeability is associated with the stability of remarriage. Openness, measured as contact with relatives, friends, and acquaintances, is associated with stability, whereas a high level of contact with helping agencies or other community organizations is associated with instability.

Loyalty Conflicts

Divided loyalty refers to the discomfort associated with having feelings of affection for one person that interferes with positive feelings felt toward another. It can also be defined as feeling torn between meeting the needs of one person rather than those of another when simultaneous demands are made. This can be manifest in many ways. For example, children may feel they are being disloyal to a biological father who does not live with them when they begin to have positive feelings for a stepfather with whom they live. Similarly, loyalty conflicts may result when children feel forced to take sides in a dispute between their divorced parents. Children report that the latter situation is stressful. Although the clinical literature commonly discusses these ideas, only two researchers have examined it empirically. Lutz (1983) questioned 103 adolescents living in stepfamilies about their feelings when one biological parent talks negatively about the other. Over 50% of the adolescents reported they had experienced this situation and almost three-quarters perceived it as stressful. A total of 43% of the adolescents reported they had experienced feeling "caught in the middle" between two biological parents and more than half (58%) reported feeling stressed by this experience. Lutz asked the teenagers how they felt about liking a step-parent more than their natural parent of the same sex. Again, 55% reported they had experienced this situation and 40% reported that the experience was stressful.

JoAnne Strother and Ed Jacobs (1984) used the same measures as Lutz to study adolescent stress. They questioned a sample of 63 high school students living in stepfamilies. Unlike Lutz, divided loyalties did not emerge as a particularly stressful problem for these teenagers. It ranked eighth in a list of 13 potentially stressful problems. Instead, these students reported that discipline caused them the most stress. Strother and Jacobs compared these findings with the responses of 100 teenagers living in first families, and found these teens also reported discipline as the most stressful area of family life. As a result, the authors concluded that problems with discipline are probably common in all types of families, regardless of parent's marital status.

In summary, we note that divided loyalty is a problem for at least some children in stepfamilies. Lutz's study of 12- to 18-year olds, and Paul Koren and his colleagues' study (1983) of 9- to 18-year olds both found that children reported negative emotions when they were caught in the middle between their quarrelling biological parents.

Resource Distribution

Another aspect of remarriage that affects spousal adjustment is the way in which resources are distributed. Several factors must be considered when comparing resource management and resource distribution in first versus second (or subsequent) marriages. First, when couples marry for the first time they typically develop an interdependent economic life. Even though they may encounter financial problems, the marriage itself is a single economic unit with one or both partners producing the family income. Second, economic goals tend to be constrained by the particular stage in the family life cycle the members are experiencing at the moment. For example, family financial goals in the first stage of marriage likely focus primarily upon setting up the household and buying the necessary items to function as a family. Planning for retirement or saving for children's college education are usually not part of the couple's financial decisions at this time. Thus family stages serve to guide expenditures and motivate the distribution of resources (Fishman, 1983).

When a person enters into a remarriage, financial decision-making becomes more complex. After having spent some time in independent households, remarried partners must find some compatible way to handle their two economies. This may necessitate incorporating people from two separate households and two different generations who have different and/or opposing earning, spending, and saving habits. An additional factor complicates the family economy, for as Barbara Fishman (1983) points out, financial responsibilities after remarriage may involve three or four adults across several households. In addition, the remarried family may be experiencing several different family stages simultaneously (for example, the newly married couple stage and the adolescent child stage). These two stages may conflict in their demands for resource distribution. That means problems may arise over whether to spend money for new household items versus a teenage child's request for a used car.

Fishman (1983) interviewed 16 remarried families to determine how they managed their economic resources. From in-depth interviews she derived two distinct patterns of financial distribution: a *common pot* and a *two pot pattern*. The common pot meant that partners pooled all available resources and distributed them according to family members' needs regardless of relationship—child or stepchild. Families who adopted the common pot pattern shared two characteristics: (a) they usually operated with limited funds and therefore had to focus on current financial needs, and (b) at least one of the partners had an ex-spouse who failed consistently to make child support payments for his or her biological child(ren). Because resources were usually scarce in common pot families, this pattern of economics usually improved the standard of living for both spouses, compared to what each experienced before remarriages.

In the two pot pattern resources were distributed first on the basis of biological connections and only secondarily on the basis of need. Two characteristics distinguished families who adopted this distribution mode: (a) at least one and usually both partners had ex-spouses who contributed to the support of biological children, and (b) there were sufficient financial resources and thus there was some discretionary income. In these families both spouses contributed to the maintenance of the household, and each attended to the financial needs of his or her biological children. Expenses were handled separately, and there usually were no shared checking or savings accounts. The two pot system tended to maintain a tight bond between the members of a first family, irrespective of second family membership. This mode of family financing also assured a sense of autonomy and independence between the remarried partners. The most difficult challenge for two pot families was how to achieve some balance between personal economic independence and step-family cohesion.

Addressing issues more typical of common pot families, Ann Goetting (1982) suggests that "the problem of finances in remarriage is not so much one of insufficient funds as it is one of financial instability and resource distribution" (p. 220). She cites 1978 Census Bureau data that document the sporadic nature of child support payments to remarried wives. In 1978 only 43% of remarried wives reported always having received their support payments, as opposed to 51% of divorced but not remarried wives. A second source of economic instability for remarried couples comes from not knowing what unexpected requests or demands will come from the husband's ex-spouse, who typically has custody of his children.

Kenneth Kressel (1985) reports even gloomier figures illustrating the instability of support payments to mothers with physical custody of children. He writes that noncompliance of support payments increases over time: By the third year after divorce the rate of nonpayment is 60%; by the fifth year it is around 70%-80%.

Limited resources also means the remarried couple may begin their new marriage in the same house that was once shared with a new spouse's former mate. This can be a source of discomfort since memories of the former marriage pervade the house and the neighborhood. A new spouse may find it hard to feel "at home" in a setting decorated, furnished, or financed by his or her partner and another man or woman (Burgoyne and Clark, 1982).

Finances generate conflict between newly remarried spouses. An obvious way to decrease the potential for conflict is to discuss finances prior to marriage. However, research shows that remarried couples are reluctant to do this. Lillian Messinger (1976) interviewed 70 couples who reported they were reluctant to discuss financial matters with each other before marriage. Over half of the 22 couples interviewed by Elizabeth Dolan and Jean Louen (1985) confessed that financial stress had contributed to the breakup of their first marriage, yet most of them were not willing to discuss finances with their future spouses before remarrying.

Just as money must be distributed, so must other resources, including time, space, and affection. The needs of a newly remarried couple to spend time alone may compete with the needs of the entire family group to spend time in family activities. Also, as the number in the family increases via remarriage, the time available to give to individual members becomes more limited. Take the case of a child whose biological parents remarried, adding two sets of stepgrandparents to the child's family. Should all four sets of grandparents desire the child's company, choices must be made to accommodate individual needs.

The distribution of space can influence interaction between stepfamily members. A home that adequately housed a family of three after separation and divorce, but after remarriage must accommodate six people, represents another example of resource distribution. A child who never had to share his or her bedroom suddenly may have to share this space.

Although we like to think that the affection received from a loved one has no limits, some people feel threatened and vulnerable when suddenly they think they have to compete with new family members for a share of a loved one's affection. By definition, if not in reality, new family members have the right to that love. Since there are no rules about how affection gets distributed among new stepfamily members, people do not know what to expect. One consequence of this ambiguity and fear of loss of love can be conflict and hostility between new stepfamily members.

In summary, remarried couples have several different patterns to choose from in deciding the way they will distribute their financial resources. Their choice may depend on the amount of resources available, as well as the strength of ties to a "first" family. Further, although remarried spouses realize the strain that financial difficulties can have on a marriage, few are able to discuss money matters and financial planning before remarriage. The distribution of resources other than money also can be problematic for remarried couples. Resources such as time, space, and affection must be allocated and equitably distributed before all family members feel contented with the new living arrangements.

CONCLUSION

The following quote from a 25-year-old doctor's office receptionist, married two years, illustrates with feeling one way that first marriage and remarriage differ.

Ours is a situation where my husband's wife left him for another man. It left him with bitter feelings that sometimes inadvertently carry over into our marriage. I also know that he still and always will love his ex-wife very much. And even though he loves me, I feel sometimes that if she would have him, he would be happier married to her. And even though I realize that this isn't a "healthy" attitude, I compete with his first wife in things I do in everyday living—for instance, wondering if I keep house as well as she or cook as well, etc. Marriage is difficult enough without these added stresses. It has been difficult for me falling in love with a man that was previously married. I guess I've always wanted to be someone's *first* and only choice! If I had the chance to do it all again, I don't think I would have become seriously involved with him when he told me, "I've been married before."

Of course, all remarriages are not so affected by one spouse's failure to loosen his or her attachment (in this case a bitter attachment) to a prior spouse. However, it remains a genuine problem for some. Families that harbor the "myths" of instant love and instant adjustment, and that attempt to recreate the lost nuclear family also postpone the eventual adjustments that settle them into a family unit. Adjustment eventually includes recognizing and appreciating the special attributes and strengths, as well as the weaknesses, of a stepfamily. Those that fail to meet the challenge are more likely the 60% who face divorce again. For, as Furstenberg and Spanier (1984: 439-440) noted among the Centre County, Pennsylvania, remarrieds they studied, "they were prepared to dissolve their second marriage if it did not work out. Regardless of how unattractive they considered this eventuality, the great majority indicated that after having endured a first marriage to the breaking point, they were unwilling to be miserable again simply for the sake of preserving the union."

On the positive side, the experience of having had a prior marriage is translated by some spouses into making an extra effort to make the second one successful. This sentiment is reflected in the words of a 29-year-old hair-stylist, married 4 years:

My wife's first marriage was so bad that she tries all that much harder to make this one work.

And this from a 28-year-old aluminum applicator, married 4½ years:

My wife's ex was a real puke. (Still is.) This made me look good, even though I'm no prize.

Before closing this chapter we raise again the issue of satisfaction in marriage that coexists with a wide array of problems as reported by couples and children in remarried families. We need to emphasize one important point. Not many family researchers ask spouses and children in *first* marriages about the particular problems they face. Thus when attention is focused on the problems in remarried families, there is no clear basis for comparison. It may be that a couple's interpersonal relationship, money problems, discipline of children, and fighting parents who speak ill of one another are problems that surface in first marriages, too. It also may be that couples have the ability to differentiate between what happens within the marital relationship versus what is going on in the family. A couple may be having severe problems with children or an ex-spouse but be able to keep these types of problems separate from their feelings about the marriage and each other. Family problems, therefore, do not come to mind when asked about satisfaction with the marriage.

Several writers suggest that it is wise to focus on the strengths rather than the problems of remarriage (Furstenberg and Spanier, 1984; Strother and Jacobs, 1984). We concur with this recommendation. We do not want to exaggerate the difficulties remarried couples face, leaving an impression of despair and hopelessness. On the other hand—the redivorce statistics plainly convey the message that over half of remarried couples do not successfully cope with the problems that emerge after remarriage. Since children are viewed by many to be a primary source of the difficulty, in the following chapter we examine the effects of remarriage on children. We also address the power that stepchildren have to break up the marriage.

DISCUSSION QUESTIONS

(1) Cohabitation before remarriage does not seem to be related to marital satisfaction. Discuss why you think this is so.

(2) How might members of remarried families foster the development of clear family boundaries?

(3) Discuss the ways that custody arrangements influence loyalty conflicts.

(4) Although resource distribution is believed to complicate remarriage, what might be some of the positive outcomes of a new distribution of resources?

RELATED READINGS

GOETTING, A. (1982) "The six stations of remarriage: developmental tasks of remarriage after divorce." Family Relations 31: 213-222.

DUBERMAN, L. (1975) The Reconstituted Family: A Study of Remarried Couples and Their Children. Chicago: Nelson-Hall.

MACKLIN, E. (1983) "Non-marital cohabitation: an overview," pp. 49-74 in E. D. Macklin and R. H. Rubin (eds.) Contemporary Families and Alternative Lifestyles. Beverly Hills, CA: Sage.

CHAPTER
5

The Children

Once there was a gentleman who married, for his second wife, the proudest and haughtiest woman ever seen. By her former husband she had two daughters who were exactly like her. Her new husband had a daughter, too, by an earlier marriage, but this child was the sweetest and best creature one could imagine.

As soon as the wedding ceremony was over, the wife began to show her true nature. She could not bear it that her husband's pretty daughter with all her goodness made her own daughters appear the more hateful. She began to use her for the meanest housework. She ordered her to scour the pots and to scrub the tables and the floors. She gave her a wretched straw pallet for a bed in the garret while her own daughters lay below upon soft new beds and had full length mirrors in which to admire themselves.

The poor girl bore all this with patience and dared not tell her father, for she saw that he was ruled completely by his new wife. . .
                                                                —Cinderella

WHEN FOLK TALES about mistreated stepchildren such as Cinderella were first told, being a stepchild was not an uncommon event. In an earlier chapter we discussed the incidence of remarriage in the past. You will recall that even though the current remarriage rate is similar to the earlier one, a primary difference is that most remarriages today follow first marriages that were ended by divorce instead of death. Thus one of the major differences that distinguishes stepchildren of the past from those of the present is the way the majority of children "lose" their biological parent. This is reflected in the term *step,* which originally meant orphan. The stories of Cinderella, Snow White, and Hansel and Gretel are more likely the first source of knowledge about being a stepchild for children today, rather than actual experience. Nevertheless, a large minority of today's children have a reasonable probability of experiencing stepfamily life firsthand. In 1980 it was estimated that there were 2.3 million households with stepparents who were raising stepchildren (Cherlin and McCarthy, 1985). Estimates of the probability of experiencing a parental divorce are about 33% (Glick, 1984). Sandra Hofferth (1985) estimates that 64% of white children and 89% of black children will live at some point in their lives in a single-parent household by the time they reach the age of 17. Of these, more than half will gain a stepparent when the mother or father with whom they reside remarries. This chapter explores the effects on children of living in a stepfamily, beginning with a discussion of child custody practices.

CUSTODY DECISIONS AND PRACTICES

Child custody practices have changed over the past 150 years, from a "parental rights" premise to a "tender years" doctrine to a "best interests of the child" policy. The parental rights premise regarded children as the property of their father, whereas the tender years doctrine entrusted the care of (young) children to their mother. The doctrine of best interests of the child has translated into an equal rights doctrine, wherein both parents have equal rights and responsibilities for minor children and neither parent's share is superior. This latter ruling is better known as joint custody.

Father Rights

From Roman law into ninteenth-century England and America, the father's right to the custody of his children was almost absolute. Under common law children were considered to be a father's property. Under his guardianship children were entitled to support, education, and religious training, and he was entitled to their labor and service (Derdeyn, 1976). The link between provision of support and custody is illustrated with this excerpt from an 1891 law text: "As the first duty to support the child rests on the father, he is prima facie and before all others... entitled to the custody" (Bishop, 1891: 453). This point is illustrated again by an 1840 custody decision that "a positive unfitness in the father must be shown before children can be withheld or withdrawn from his charge" (Ahrenfeldt v. Ahrenfeldt, 1840: 501). Mothers were not viewed as fit guardians since they were seen as needing protection themselves.

Only gradually, with the advent of the industrial revolution and the social changes that accompanied it, did mothers begin to gain custody rights. Andre Derdeyn (1976: 1371) describes the changes this way:

> Women began to vote, to own property in their own right, and to be gainfully employed in great numbers. At the same time, the country's new interest in children began to be manifested by the development of public education, children's aid societies... and child labor laws.... Not only did women start to develop more rights and more economic competence, but society, influenced by early interest in child development, stressed the importance of maternal care.

Mothers first won custody of very young children. Such custody was seen as a temporary exemption to the rule. Custody was awarded to the mothers of infants or toddlers (presumably those who were still nursing), and custody reverted to fathers when children reached the age of four, or sometimes age seven. Both girls and boys, but especially the latter, were given back to the care and custody of their fathers, who were viewed as the proper persons to administer discipline and moral guidance to children.

Mother Custody

In the early twentieth century, mothers were increasingly awarded custody under the principle of the "tender years" doctrine. This doctrine held that the well-being of children was enhanced if they were kept in their mother's care. Several factors influenced this change. Derdeyn (1976: 1372) summarizes these as follows:

> In addition to women's generally increasing rights and economic capability, child support from former spouses became more consistently available . . . mother's right to custody was a moral one based on a developing cultural assumption that the woman was better suited to caring for children.

Over time the policy of mother custody was eventually given preference. By 1960 mothers were given custody in over 90% of contested cases (Derdeyn, 1976), an estimate that prevails today.

The phrase "best interests of the child" was introduced into state statute in 1925. Here the intention was the child's best interest as the first criterion for placement. This policy was intended to shift the focus away from the conflicting parents in order to protect the child. It resulted in an inclination or "presumption for" maternal custody. Thus until about 1970 mother custody was the preferred placement (Luepnitz, 1982). As the struggle for social equality pervaded American society, the legal climate also was changing. "Between 1969 and 1975 nine states passed legislation explicitly stipulating that the sex of the parent should not be a factor in determining custody" (Weitzman, 1985: 466).

Joint Custody

In 1980 California became the first state to adopt a joint custody preference. Law was established to maintain the child's ties to both parents. Joint custody is variously called shared custody, cocustody, and coparenting. California's policy also encourages parents to work out their own custody arrangements; if they need assistance because of irreconcilable differences there are court affiliated mediators and counselors to help. The doctrine has proved to be popular. According to Lenore Weitzman (1985), by 1985 at least some form of joint custody legislation had been adopted in 30 states. She summarizes four alternative forms of joint custody legislation:

(1) *Joint custody as an option.* This is the least specific of joint custody forms, and it permits the court to order joint custody for parents who have not requested it.

(2) *Joint custody when parents agree.* This statute permits joint custody only when both parents request it. According to Weitzman, these laws follow the growing consensus that the agreement of the parties is a prerequisite for making joint custody work.

(3) *Joint custody at one party's request.* This policy permits the judge to award joint custody when only one parent requests it. Weitzman feels this can be detrimental to children because it places children at the center of their parent's conflict.

(4) *Joint custody preference or presumption.* These are the most coercive forms of joint custody because they require judges to give preference to joint custody. Joint custody presumption is the strongest of the two, since it assumes that joint custody is in the child's best interests. In order to overcome this presumption, a parent is required to prove that joint custody would be detrimental to the child. In these cases sole custody is the exception and requires special justification.

In actuality, the way in which joint custody is translated into daily living arrangements varies considerably. One study of 50 divorced couples reported that no two joint arrangements were alike, but four general patterns emerged: (a) children split the day between two homes; (b) children spent varying amounts of time during the week between two homes; (c) children split the year living in two homes (usually the summer and one or two major holidays in one home and the rest of the time with the other parent); and (d) children lived alternate years in two homes (Luepnitz, 1982). These alternatives all center on joint *physical* custody. *Legal* custody means the "child's legal custodian is responsible for the education and welfare of a child under 18; he or she may control the religious training the child is or is not taught, and has the power to authorize medical care for the child" (Weitzman, 1985: 227). Legal custody does not specify who the child lives with. Joint legal custody means that both parents have the right to be involved in making important decisions about the child's upbringing, schooling, religious training, health care, and so on.

Accurate reporting on a child's custodial/living arrangements involves an awkward terminology. That is, the customary term to describe a child's living situation would be to say he or she is in a mother-custody or father-custody home. However, that term is not accurate if the child's biological parents have joint legal custody but the physical custody of the child is with the mother. To eliminate inaccurate implications, we use the term *residential* to mean living arrangements, and *custody* to mean the child's legal custodial situation. Unfortunately, the consequence of this precision is a sometimes cumbersome phrasing.

An excellent study by Weitzman (1985) shows that the California no-fault divorce legislation did not result in any significant increases in father requests for child custody. In fact, even the new joint custody law has effected little change in custody awards. Weitzman (1985: 250) suggests that what has occurred in California is a change in labeling:

> Arrangements that would have been called "liberal visitation" before 1980, under the old law, are now called "joint custody." The shift may have important psychological consequences for fathers who can now define themselves as joint parents after divorce, but it has not changed the day-to-day arrangements for the care of most children.

The Ideal versus the Real: Joint Custody Versus Visiting

One of the concerns of family scholars as well as those in the helping professions is the large number of children who are growing up without the continued involvement of their biological father. Information on the amount of child-father contact after divorce overwhelmingly confirms that, over time, father involvement diminishes in the majority of cases. One of the earliest studies of divorce documented this tendency (Goode, 1965), and researchers have continued to affirm it. E. Mavis

Hetherington and Martha and Roger Cox (1976) conducted a two-year longitudinal study of children of divorce and found that father-child contact decreased steadily over time. A recent national study found that nearly 50% of the children in the study had not seen their non-residential parent in the past five years. Of those children who had visited this parent in the past five years, 20% had not seen him or her in the past year. Only 16% of these children saw their absent parent an average of once a week (Furstenberg et al., 1983). Furstenberg and Spanier's (1984) study of Pennsylvania remarried couples supports the findings of other studies, again suggesting that father-child contact decreases over time. Their data also suggested that contact was reduced if a remarriage took place. When neither parent was married, two-thirds of the nonresidential parents visited with their children at least a few times a month. When one of the partners was married, the proportion dropped to 40%. When both parents had remarried the proportion who visited their children a few times a month dropped further to 34%.

Similar findings are reported by Walter Tropf (1984) in a study of 101 divorced fathers. Here again visitation decreased after divorce, decreased more after the father's remarriage, and still more after the remarriage of the ex-wife. Tropf noted, however, that although frequency dropped after remarriage, duration of visits increased: Children visited less frequently but stayed for longer visits. Tropf acknowledged that a decrease in visiting frequency did not necessarily denote a decline in father's interest or involvement. "The findings on phone calls, plus the increase in visiting length accompanying the decline in frequency, indicate a reordering of roles" (1984: 70). However, in this study an increasing number of fathers ceased contact with their children altogether: 12% never visited their children after the divorce. After their own remarriage, 23% ceased visitation, and 31% did so after the remarriage of their ex-wife.

Weitzman's (1985) California study showed the same gradual decrease in contact between nonresidential fathers and their children. What's more, California court records show that 23% of fathers did not see their children at all after the divorce.

In contrast to the general trends, one study that examined the behavior of parents who held joint legal custody found a higher rate of involvement with children. In her study of 41 joint custody families, Ahrons (1981) found that about two-thirds of the nonresidential parents saw their children at least once a week or more.

Most studies of nonresidential mothers report that visitation is both more regular and more frequent than nonresidential father visitation. In the Furstenberg and Spanier study reported earlier, 86% of the children who did not live with their biological mothers had contact with them in the past year. Only 48% of children with nonresidential fathers had such contact. Of nonresidential mothers, 31% saw their children at least once a week compared to 16% of nonresidential fathers.

We must interpret the figures relating to mother-visiting with some caution, however, since in most studies the number of nonresidential mothers is quite small (there were only 35 visiting mothers in the Furstenberg and Spanier study). However, the trends are consistent. Mothers visit their nonresidential children more frequently than fathers.

We should note that in some studies the high rate of father involvement may be affected by the way the samples were selected. The Ahrons study selected samples in order to examine family interaction in a binuclear family. Thus families included in the study held joint legal custody. An incentive to cooperate with a study of mother custody families was built into a study conducted by clinicians Judith Wallerstein and Joan Kelly (1980). These researchers found a high degree of father contact after divorce. This may have been because the researchers offered the study families a six-week prevention program designed to help children and adolescents cope with divorce in exchange for their participation (Kelly, 1981).

Age of children and geographic distance are said to influence visitation. The national study designed by Furstenberg, Peterson, and Zill that was reported on earlier, however, found that sex and age of child did not seem to affect contact with father. Residential closeness was a salient factor. Weekly contact was reduced by half when the father lived over an hour's drive from the child. However, visitation rates of "once a month or more" were not affected by geographic distance (Furstenberg et al., 1983). It seems that geographic closeness facilitates visitation, but does not determine it. Tropf (1984) examined the differences in frequency of visitation of fathers living within 150 miles of the child and those living farther away. As reported earlier, he found that frequency of visitation decreased after divorce, decreased further at father's remarrige, and decreased still further upon an ex-wife's remarriage when fathers lived within 150 miles. A similar, but more dramatic, pattern of decreased visitation occured when the father lived more than 150 miles away.

The evidence is clear that the marital status of one or both former spouses influences the frequency of contact between children and their nonresidential parent in a negative way. There also is a connection between visitation, remarriage, and financial support of children. Furstenberg et al. (1983) found that fathers who paid some child support were more likely to see their children on a regular basis than fathers who did not. Tropf (1984) found that requests for additional support were more likely met if the father had remarried, but were reduced if his ex-wife remarried.

These findings may be explained in several ways. Remarriage means that energy, attention, and resources must be divided among prior and current families. Redirecting resources to a new family means there is less for members of the prior family, children included. Should the remarriage also include children, the demands on resources multiply. Also, a new spouse may not encourage the continued contact with a former spouse and children, seeing such contact as a constant reminder of the past. There is a strong desire to "put the past behind us" among remarried couples (Visher and Visher, 1979). Some ex-spouses engage in conflict over support payments, visitation, child-rearing practice, and so forth. Poor relations between former spouses can readily discourage and dishearten fathers' attempts to maintain a relationship with their children (Fox, 1985). Further, the visits between fathers and their children can be painful due in part to their intensity, brevity, and insufficiency. Guilt feelings on the part of the father may result. When negative feelings accompany or follow visitation, it is likely that contact will decrease.

The other half of the binuclear family, residential mothers, also report problems. They say that children are unruly and emotionally drained after visiting their nonresidential fathers (Weiss, 1979). They complain that the father commonly fails to enforce rules and offers only "good times" instead of enforcing the rules necessary for ordinary child rearing. Visitation sometimes means seeing a former spouse when one would prefer not to have that contact. Consciously or unconsciously, mothers may act in ways to disrupt or discourage continued contact.

Custody and Residence Shifting

There is no precise information on the number of children whose legal custody changes or who shift their residence from one parent's home to another's, or on why these changes are made. Some studies offer limited information regarding the prevalence of such shifts. One noteworthy characteristic associated with children's shift of residence is that such changes do not necessarily involve all children in the family. One or more children may continue to live with one parent while another child moves in with the other parent. In a study of 517 mothers without custody Geoffrey Grief (1986) reported 61% of the mothers had physical custody when the marriage ended, but subsequently lost it or gave it up. Of these mothers 26% had split physical custody, with at least one child under age 18 living with them. In another study Grief (1985) found that 19.6% of his father-custody sample (N = 1136) had children living with them because their former wife could no longer handle them. Similar estimates are suggested by Furstenberg and Spanier (1984) who reported that almost 20% of the Centre County, Pennsylvania, respondents experienced a change in custody arrangements. Julie Fulton (1979) reported a 33% shift rate in her study of Minnesota divorces. In a study of single-parent fathers, Barbara Risman (1986) reported that among 141 fathers, 62% said they had little choice in assuming responsibility for the care of their children because their wives had deserted, died, or refused the responsibility. A total of 18% had negotiated for custody while they were still married, and 20% had obtained custody by legal action against the wishes of their wives.

Overall, fathers are unlikely to obtain sole custody, regardless of the life conditions of the mother. Fathers are somewhat more likely to have custody of all children if their former partners have remarried. They are also more likely to gain custody if all children in the family are boys, and least likely to have custody if all children are girls. Finally, it is estimated that about half of the fathers with custody of any children have custody of only part of the sibling group, and about half have custody of all the children in the family (Spanier and Glick, 1981).

Many times, a change in residence occurs several years after an initial custody award. The reasons for these changes are not straightforward and may not always be for the good of the child. Behavior may be motivated by the wish to disrupt the new marriage of an ex-spouse, or a new stepmother may have a "rescue fantasy" and wish to provide better mothering for her stepchildren than she perceives their biological mother provides. Other reasons for child shifting include illness in a custodial parent, a desire on the part of children to move, a mother's desire to further her education or career that involves a large time commitment, or a mother's feeling that she cannot handle a particular child.

The following statements serve to illustrate the reactions of three parents about child shifting. First, a mother's perspective on her child's move to his father's home, followed by the comments of two fathers about their children's moves.

(Mother, age 27, homemaker, married 6 years): One of the biggest problems seems to be the children. Accepting the stepparent. Once you have convinced the child that the stepparent does not wish to take the place of the real parent, tension eases and the child begins to love the stepparent for himself. Often children of this age don't understand that they can feel love for a stepparent without losing the love of his real parent. This was a serious problem with our oldest boy until recently. He has been living with his real father for 2 months and is ready to return home. Now he is secure about his feelings for his real father and stepfather. We think this separation will ultimately bring us closer together and now we can stay together where we now *all* want to be. This was the hardest thing we had to do, but we felt we had to "let him go before we could bring him back."

(Father, age 41, salesman, married 5½ years): I am very pleased with my marriage. My two younger children lived with us by choice for a period of time, the girl returned to her mother by choice after 9 months, the boy by consensus after 16 months. My wife and I are both in career situations and lacked the time to supervise properly. The children brought problems into our marriage and did not respond to *our* expectations. We both made our best effort to have a family that worked well, but did not have available adequate supervision. I was raised by a stepfather who was without a doubt the best, but I never realized it until I was an adult, and stepchildren like stepparents can be very cruel and very cold with very little effort.

(Father, age 37, carpet cleaner, married 4 years): We have a total of 7 children in our marriage. Four from my wife and three from myself. Not all these children get along super but for the most part are doing OK together. There are two children who don't live with us anymore. One needed to be with her mother. Seems to be OK. The other ran away. Couldn't handle her own problems. Nine people together from a marriage and most of them benefiting from the union.

CONSEQUENCES OF
REMARRIAGE FOR CHILDREN

The Adjustment of Children
to Parental Remarriage

Empirical findings suggest that the age of the child at the time of parental divorce and remarriage, sex of the child, and sex of the stepparent are important factors for understanding and predicting the influence of family change on children.

A few studies have investigated the relationship between age of child and children's adjustment to parental remarriage. Wallerstein and Kelly's (1980) study mentioned earlier suggests that school—aged children are particularly vulnerable to the stress associated with the remarriage of a residential parent. Their findings are supported by others (Rosenberg, 1965; Kaplan and Pokorny, 1971). Parental remarriage that occurs early in the child's life (before age five) has been found to have positive effects on the child's I.Q. and school performance.

Early studies generally neglected to study sex differences, but more recent research has consistently found that boys in stepfamilies have fewer adjustment problems and less negative outcomes than do girls. Several studies have reported that girls have more difficulty in their relationship with their stepparents than do boys, particularly with stepmothers (Clingempeel and Segal, 1986; Peterson and Zill, 1986). Lucile Duberman (1975) reported that stepmothers and stepdaughters have more problematic relationships than stepfathers and stepsons.

In a study asking adolescent members of stepfamilies about stressful aspects of stepfamily life, Lutz (1983) found boys with stepfathers reported less stress associated with living in a stepfamily than did girls. Clingempeel and Segal's (1986) recent study emphasizes the association between good relations in stepfamilies and psychological adjustment. They found that the more positive this relationship was (between stepmother and stepchild) the better the psychological adjustment. This finding was particularly pronounced for girls.

It has been suggested that the stepparent-stepchild relation may be influenced by the quality of the marital relationship. In Brand and Clingempeel's (1985) study, remarried mothers with good marital adjustment had daughters who reported less positive relationships with their stepfathers. In stepmother families, the more positive the stepmother's marital adjustment, the less positive their relationship with their stepdaughter. This finding was not true for stepmothers with stepsons.

Although the current empirical evidence suggests that girls in stepfamilies may be at greater "risk" than boys, this conclusion should be considered with caution. The majority of these studies have used small, middle-class, Caucasian samples. However, one study with a large, random sample of respondents did affirm these findings (Peterson and Zill, 1986). Still, more studies are needed before we can trust this finding about sex differences.

Academic Achievement and Cognitive Functioning

Several studies have examined the influence of remarriage on the academic performance and/or cognitive functioning of children. Four studies concur that being reared in a stepparent family does not negatively influence either the academic achievement or the cognitive functioning of children. For example, no differences were found in school grades for children reared in stepfamilies compared to those reared in first families (Bohannan and Yahraes, 1979). John Santrock's (1972) study reported similar findings in a sample of grade school children. I.Q. and achievement scores were the same for boys living with stepfathers and those living with biological fathers. Boys living with stepfathers also were found to have higher I.Q. and achievement scores than boys living in single-parent households. Living with a stepfather, however, did not have the same effects for girls in Santrock's study. Girls in stepfather families performed significantly lower on achievement tests than girls in intact first families. There were no differences in girls' performance when comparing girls in stepfather families and girls in single-parent families.

Self-Esteem, Self-Confidence, and Personality Variables

A child's sense of "self" has been a popular topic of investigation in stepfamily research. The majority of studies found no differences in self-concept and self-image between children reared in first families, single-parent households, and stepparent families. Two studies found that children reared in stepfamilies had lower self-images than children reared in first families. Of these two, only one strongly demonstrated that children in stepfamilies had lower self-images. The other found self-esteem was negative only if parental remarriage had occurred when the child was older than age eight. Overall, these studies have failed to consider the variety of factors beyond family structure that likely influence self-esteem; factors such as family size, length of time in remarriage, and so on.

Psychological Functioning

Many researchers have been interested in studying the psychological functioning of children in stepfamilies. However, comparing the findings from one study with those of another is difficult because researchers have measured psychological functioning in a variety of ways. We believe the use of diverse measures and methods contributes to the conflicting findings.

Harvey Oshman and Martin Manosevitz (1976) found that males in father-present families (both first and step-) had a higher psychological functioning than males in father-absent families. One characteristic of this study was that the males had lived in their stepfather families for several years, suggesting that length of time in a stepfamily might be an important mediator of any possible negative effects of remarriage on boys.

Most studies assessing psychological functioning by measuring frequency of psychosomatic complaints found no difference between children reared in stepfamilies and those reared in other types of families. However, there is little recent data on general psychological functioning. More study is needed on this particular topic before general conclusions can be drawn.

Family Relationships

Overall, it becomes clear after reviewing the literature that the relationships within stepfamilies are not terribly different from those in other families. Similar issues face children and parents in all types of families. The nature of these issues, however, may be different due to the complexity of remarriage and kinship relationships, and the "newness" of family rituals, routines, and habits.

Ganong and Coleman (1984: 400) reviewed the studies that compared family relationships in stepfamilies and other types of families. They summarize the findings from several studies this way:

> No differences were found in relationships with stepfathers . . . perceptions of parental happiness . . . perception of amount of family conflict . . . socioemotional relationships between mothers and daughters . . . sharing of household tasks . . . reciprocal confiding, supportiveness, and trust between mothers and daughters . . . positive family relationships . . . and observed stepparent-child and parent-child interactions. . . . Wilson et al. (1975) found no differences in adult family relationships between adults raised in stepfather families and adults raised in nuclear families. Most stepchildren reported liking stepparents (stepfathers as well as stepmothers) and getting along well with them.

On the other hand, there are some studies that do report poorer adjustment in stepfamilies. As suggested earlier, the relationship between stepparent and stepchild is more negative than the one with a residential biological parent. Less affection is reported between stepparents and stepchildren, and stepchildren see the stepparent in a negative light (Bowerman and Irish, 1962; Halprin and Smith, 1983). One recent study on the effects of stepfamily interaction on child well-being suggests that children of divorce and remarriage exhibited more stress and more disruptive behavior than children in the general population (Jacobson, forthcoming; Peterson and Zill, 1986). We are cautious, however, not to interpret this as meaning stepchildren need psychological treatment.

It has been suggested that the stepparent-stepchild relationship is central to expressions of satisfaction with one's remarried family (Crosbie-Burnett, 1984). Further, the quality of the stepparent-stepchild relationship appears to be a better predictor of child adjustment than the quality of the relationship with the nonresidential biological parent (Furstenberg and Selzer, 1983; Furstenberg et al., 1983). This is a consistent finding across the majority of studies regardless of sample size. For example, a recent study by Pink and Wampler (1985) compared the responses from 28 stepfamilies with the responses from 28 first-marriage families on measures of family functioning and the quality of the stepfather-adolescent relationship. Their findings indicate that the ratings from the mother, stepfather, and adolescent were lower in family cohesion and adaptability and lower in quality in the stepfather-adolescent relationship than that reported by members of first families. The findings did not hold true for the mother-adolescent relationship.

Studies have examined other aspects of the stepparent-stepchild relationship. For example, research by Clingempeel et al. (1984) reported lower scores on dimensions of love and higher scores on dimensions of detachment for stepchildren, stepparents, and biological parents when they rated the stepfather-stepdaughter relationship. In this study girls were found to emit less positive verbal communication and more negative problem-solving behaviors toward their stepparents than boys. Stepparents did not differ in their response toward either their stepdaughters or stepsons. Similar findings were reported in another study by these psychologists (Clingempeel et al., 1985). Here, however, the researchers were interested in determining the possible effects of structural complexity on stepparent-stepchild interaction. Findings revealed that simple (wife had custody of a child from a previous marriage and husband had no children) and complex (wife had custody of a child from a previous marriage and husband was the father of a noncustodial child) stepfather families did not differ on any of the measures of love detachment, positive-negative verbal communication, and problem-solving behaviors.

Other Social Relationships

Most studies of the influence of remarriage and stepparenting on children's social interaction with friends, peers, and in other institutional settings suggest that stepchildren do not have any more trouble than other children do. Again, Ganong and Coleman (1984: 108) have best summarized these findings:

> Stepchildren did not differ from nuclear family children in peer relationships . . . delinquent behaviors . . . delinquent companions . . . drug use . . . school behaviors . . . and church attendance.

The findings from Furstenberg, Nord, Peterson, and Zill's 1983 National Survey of Children suggest less positive outcomes for stepchildren. These researchers conclude that children reared in stepfamilies are more vulnerable to all kinds of behavior problems than children reared in families that have not experienced divorce. Some earlier studies support the results from the National Children's Survey. For example, Barbara Dahl, Hamilton McCubbin, and Gary Lester (1976) found poorer social adjustment in stepchildren, and Shepard Kellam, Margaret Ensminger, and Jay Turner (1977) concluded that children being reared in stepfamilies are almost as "at risk" in social adaptation as children being reared in mother-custody single-parent households. These two studies were conducted with newly established stepfamilies. The National Survey of Children data demonstrate that the "at risk" concern can be applied even to children in stepfamilies that have survived the early stages of stepfamily formation.

In summary, it is still too soon to draw firm conclusions about the impact of remarriage on children's development. What we can say is that there may be some potential for risk and careful attention must be paid to children who are subjected to parental divorce and remarriage. Most marital status transitions occur within a relatively short period of time, forcing children to adjust and adapt to a multitude of changes rather quickly. It may be that the rapidity of change rather than the change itself is a primary influence on the outcomes of such change for the children involved. This question has not been thoroughly explored. In terms of the overall effects of remarriage on children, we quote Furstenberg et al.'s (1983: 667) summary of the situation: "The increasingly common pattern of divorce and remarriage is profoundly altering the practice of parenthood. The experience of growing up has probably changed as much in the past several decades as in any comparable period in American history."

CHILDREN'S POWER TO
BREAK UP THE MARRIAGE

Several researchers have reported that the divorce rate is higher in remarriages with stepchildren (Becker et al., 1977; Cherlin, 1978; White and Booth, 1985). There are at least three reasons that this may be true. First, the presence of children makes adjustment harder for a remarried couple. To illustrate, read the words of a 29-year-old woman married 5½ years:

> My husband's kids are from two different marriages. Two live with one [ex-wife] and one with the other. I have no kids and we don't want anymore. The two oldest lived with us for 1½ years and I about went crazy, but things worked out and they are gone and life is great! My marriage is wonderful and we are really happy. I think we'll keep each other.

We do not know why the children were problematic in this particular marriage, but some probable reasons have been discussed in earlier chapters. We do know that children limit a couple's privacy and the opportunity for intimacy. We know that stepmothers have a particularly difficult time parenting other women's children. We also know that remarried couples with children must accommodate to their marriage at the same time they are dealing with family matters.

It is important to differentiate between *marriage* and *family*. Although a couple may see eye-to-eye on matters that concern their behavior and personal relationship, they may differ in marked ways in their perceptions of what constitutes "good" child behavior, or rules that children "ought to" follow. They may also differ markedly in what they believe to be a proper means of disciplining when the rules are broken. First-married partners may also have disagreements about these aspects of child rearing, but a major difference is that the child in a stepfamily is not the biological offspring of both spouses. Unless the child was living with a never-married mother he or she has a history of being parented by another "father" or "mother."

Second, the discipline of children is a source of conflict between remarried spouses. There is little dispute that discipline of children is among the most frequently cited areas of difficulty reported by remarried adults, and adolescents share this perception. Discipline refers to the establishment and enforcement of family rules. It is not uncommon for a stepparent to feel that changes need to be made in the way things were done in the "old" family, and to set new rules with different expectations for children's behavior. In one study 80% of the adolescents reported they had experienced firsthand this type of discipline. They had to "adjust to living with a new set of rules from a stepparent," "accept discipline from a stepparent," and "deal with the expectations of a stepparent." These situations were judged to be stressful by the adolescents (Lutz, 1983).

Disciplining children is also stressful for adults. Because of the emotional attachment parents have to children it is very difficult to arbitrate between one's child and new spouse over matters of discipline and types or severity of punishment. This is confounded by the interpretation of behavior. Often it is not so much a matter of the actual behavior of the child but the motive behind the behavior that is important. For example, the behavior of a 16-year-old adolescent boy who takes the family car without permission may be viewed quite differently by the boy's parent and stepparent. Both may agree that the behavior was against the rules but they may disagree about the motive, his moral character, or the importance of following through with punishment under all circumstances. Different interpretations can result in conflict and disunity between parent and stepparent. Further, the parent and child can team together against the stepparent.

Third, although children typically have no say in their parent's decision to remarry and form a new family in the first place, they do have incredible power to break it up. Children can create divisiveness between spouses and siblings by acting in ways that accentuate differences between them. Children have the power to set parent against stepparent, siblings against parents, and stepsiblings against siblings. Finally, because a child is the link that unites the binuclear family, he or she has the capabilities to make uncomfortable comparisons between the two households, or to bring quasi kin and members of the extended family into the family's business. That interference is a potential source of conflict.

In summary, we began this rather long chapter by discussing the history of custody arrangements and defining different types of custody. The most common custodial arrangement in our time is for the children to reside with their mother and for fathers to "visit." We learned that father involvement decreases over time, especially as former spouses find new partners and remarry. Studies suggest that about 10%-25% of fathers do not contact their children at all after divorce. Nonresidential mothers tend to stay involved with their children more than nonresidential families. A child's residential status after divorce may change and he or she may move to the second parent's home. The most frequent move seems to be for adolescent boys to move from their mother's residence to their father's. It is estimated that about 11%-20% of children change residence (Ihinger-Tallman, 1985). Data on the adjustment of children to stepfamily life indicates that boys have an easier time than girls, and children in stepfather families have an easier time than children in stepmother families. The findings are somewhat mixed with regard to self-esteem, psychological functioning, family relationships, and children's other social relations. We depicted the vulnerability of children regarding their powerless position when the remarriage is contracted, but the strength of their position if they decide to pull against the parent's efforts to create cohesion and unity.

DISCUSSION QUESTIONS

(1) If we are truly to understand the influence of remarriage on children, what questions must we ask? (What holes exist in our current knowledge?)
(2) What might remarried spouses do to reduce the chances that children will negatively influence their marital relationship?
(3) Develop a profile of the child who fares best in a stepfamily situation. Do the same for the child who fares the worst.

RELATED READINGS

CLINGEMPEEL, W. G. and N. D. REPPUCCI (1982) "Joint custody after divorce: major issues and goals for research." Psychology Bulletin 91: 102-129.

LUEPNITZ, D.A. (1982) Child Custody: A Study of Families After Divorce. Lexington, MA: D.C. Heath.

PETERSON, J. L. and N. ZILL (1986) "Marital disruption, parent-child relationships, and behavior problems in children." Journal of Marriage and the Family 48: 295-307.

CHAPTER

6

Steprelations,
Kin and
Friendship Ties

Interview with Michelle, a 20-year-old college junior. She is the youngest of five sisters, and has one stepsister. Her father sued for and won custody of the three youngest children when she was 11. She lived with her father and stepmother seven years before attending college. Her stepmother, Helen, was a teacher at the high school and the faculty advisor for the school cheerleaders. Both Michelle and her stepsister were cheerleaders.

(Interviewer): What's your stepmother like?

She's real quiet and doesn't talk much to people. Like even when I have friends over, she'll say "Hi," and things like that, but she doesn't really—it kind of changes the atmosphere cuz you're kind of afraid. . . . I don't know, we just don't get along. . . After Stephanie [her stepsister] left for college and I was the only one at home, I had a really rough senior year. She was really upset that Stephanie was gone and I was there all the time, and it was like, how come you're here and not her? . . . That's the hardest part, I've never ever really sat down and talked to her. I'm too nervous. . . . For all the kids, too; it's not like it was just me. That's why Sarah didn't want to move in. I mean, this is really bad, but to this day I think I'm the only one in the family that can even begin to get along with Helen, that's my stepmom. It's pretty bad.

(Interviewer): What about Stephanie? Is she close to her father?

She used to be when she was little, but now her father's back in Iowa. She talks to him, and stuff, more than I talk to my mom, but it's still not *that* close anymore.

(About siblings): I think all the kids care for each other a lot. We pretty much keep in contact with each other. I hear more from them than I do from my dad or my mom.

RELATIONSHIPS BETWEEN MEMBERS of stepfamilies have been described in various ways: complex, overwhelming, stressful, challenging. A common assumption is that divorce and remarriage enlarge one's pool of kin, thereby enriching the kinship network (Bohannan, 1970; Riley, 1982). Research, however, does not support this belief (Furstenberg, 1981; Furstenberg and Nord, 1985). A discussion of the unique qualities of the various steprelationships is the focus of this chapter.

STEPPARENT-STEPCHILD RELATIONSHIPS

Propinquity (nearness in place or time) goes a long way toward explaining the nature of interaction between stepparents and stepchildren. Stepparents who interact with stepchildren on a daily basis have more opportunity to develop positive emotional bonds *and* to experience conflictual relationships than stepparents who rarely see their stepchildren. One advantage of having children live in the home is that relationships, rules, and routines become normal and new habits and rituals can develop. Similarly, visiting stepchildren may feel, or can be made to feel, as if they are intruders to the stepfamily because they do not know or may forget the rules and routines. There may not be a "place" for them or their possessions in the visited household (for example, they may sleep on the couch). Later in this chapter we discuss what happens when children see themselves treated differently than siblings or stepsiblings who permanently reside in the home.

Stepparents may feel ambivalent toward visiting stepchildren. Although, on one hand they may look forward to the visits, on the other hand, feelings of disappointment may occur when the child expresses ambivalence or hostility toward them. Conversely, stepparents may see the visiting child as an intrusion to an otherwise calm family life—visits may be defined as a time to be endured and silently celebrated when over.

The literature indicates that men and women face different problems in their roles as stepparents. These difficulties are discussed in the following sections.

Common Problems of Stepfathers

Stepfathers report seeing themselves as less adequate and less competent than either their spouses or stepchildren see them (Bohannan and Yahraes, 1979). They also report feeling inadequate in their ability to maintain close physical and emotional contact with their stepchildren, more so than biological fathers (Weingarten, 1980). Findings from Duberman's (1975) study support this detached quality of the stepfather-stepchild relationship. She found that the majority of stepfathers in her sample of 88 stepfamilies did not perceive mutual love or mutual respect between themselves and their stepchildren. Only 53% of the stepfathers experienced parental feelings toward their stepchildren and acted in ways to assist their socialization.

Some stepfathers may be responsible for two sets of children simultaneously—their stepchildren and their own biological children. The influence of this dual responsibility can be stressful. Feelings of guilt surface when fathers feel they are not adequately providing for their own biological children. However, some fathers feel that when a stepfather enters the life of their children (that is, their ex-spouse remarries) the financial obligation of support should be shared between the fathers. In the study by Tropf (1984) reported earlier, 18% of fathers felt this way; 35% of the fathers commented that the stepfather should be the one *most* responsible for the financial support of stepchildren. We might believe that an even larger percentage of fathers hold this idea when we remember that less than half of all fathers make child-support payments to their nonresidential children.

What is it that fosters stepfather satisfaction? James Anderson (1982) asked 110 stepfathers about their roles. He found stepfather satisfaction was positively correlated with the amount of communication with the stepchild. Also, stepfathers who felt they were supported by their wives for their involvement and discipline of the stepchildren reported greater satisfaction with their life. Mark Hafkin (1981) found that stepfather satisfaction increased with more involvement with stepchildren when the stepfather had no children of his own. The same positive relationship was not found for stepfathers who had biological children living elsewhere. Thus whether the stepfather also is a biological father may influence his feelings of satisfaction.

As we reported in the previous chapter, sex of stepchild affects the nature of the stepfather-stepchild relationship: Girls have more difficult relations with stepfathers than do boys (Clingempeel et al., 1984; Santrock et al., 1982). In part, this may be a function of the closeness and dependence that develop during the single-parent phase—a closeness that is disrupted by remarriage.

Common Problems of Stepmothers

Although there have been only a few studies focusing on stepmother families, the evidence portrays a consistent picture. There is more confusion and problematic interaction among family members in stepmother families. Several explanations have been offered for the more problematic nature of life in this type of stepfamily. One explanation suggests that residential stepmother families may begin differently than stepfather families. Furstenberg and Nord (1985: 902) suggest that it seems likely that children living with their fathers may have been exposed to a difficult custody negotiation or may have a special history of troubled family relations.

The findings from Giles-Sims's (1985) research support this idea. She found that paternal custody typically resulted either at the time of the divorce or because the mother could no longer handle an adolescent child (usually a male). When children change residence from mother to father because mothers cannot handle a child, fathers and step-mothers gain a son or daughter who may need more supervision or discipline than is typical for most children of the same age. In particular, adolescence is a time when well-functioning families are characterized by greater flexibility and independence of members (Olson et al., 1983). In a stepfamily, flexibility may be a luxury if the adolescent was too dif-ficult for the mother to handle and is moved because he or she needs "straightening out."

Another situation that can lead to problematic stepmother family relations is when a remarried wife never anticipated becoming a full-time stepparent. A remarried woman who planned never to have children may suddenly find herself a full-time stepmother. This situa-tion is evident in the comments from a 36-year-old stepmother, married four years, who is the office manager for a health-care service:

> We have been most fortunate in our second marriage in that we've not experienced any real problems. My husband has an 11-year-old son from his first marriage. This summer it was decided that he would move from California and come live with us. I have no children and have not been around children much during my life. I certainly had no idea what a responsibility this would be nor what restriction this would put on our freedom. After about 6 months I'm feeling much better about our cur-rent situation. I guess what I'm saying is I wish I would have had some-one to talk to who had been in my same situation. Again, I'm fortunate to have an understanding husband and a very good little boy.

Janice Nadler (1976) has provided some information about the step-mother's role, comparing 24 part-time and 24 full-time stepmothers with 24 biological mothers. She examined the level of intrapersonal (within self) and interpersonal (between self and others) conflict attached to the stepmother role. Both types of stepmothers reported more intrapersonal conflict (more depression and anger) regarding family relationships than did biological mothers. Part-time stepmothers experienced less positive involvement in family relationships and reported more conflict over family life, their parent role, finances, and interaction with relatives and others in the community. However, these findings varied somewhat by the age of children. Stepmothers with younger stepchildren were found to have lower marital adjustment and more conflict with their spouse and the children than did biological mothers with younger children. Full-time stepmothers with older stepchildren were found to have greater conflict with their spouse, conflict over child rearing and discipline, and less marital satisfaction than biological mothers with older children. Finally, part-time stepmothers with older children reported more conflict between themselves and the stepchild than either part-time stepmothers with younger children or biological mothers regardless of the age of children. Thus there seem to be distinct differences between part-time and full-time stepmothers, and between both types of stepmothers and biological mothers. Further, the age of the stepchild influences the nature of interaction such that full-time stepmothers have the most difficult time, particularly those with older stepchildren. However, these findings must be interpreted cautiously because of the small sample size.

Elsa Ferri (1984) investigated stepfamily relationships among a national sample of British children, comparing children in stepfamilies with children in single-parent households and those living with both biological parents. One quarter of the girls stated explicitly that they did not get on well with their stepmothers, compared to 5% of girls in first families. Boys also reported less positive relations in stepmother families, with 16% saying they did not get along well (compared to 4% in first families).

Given that societal expectations encourage women to assume primary care responsibilities for children, stepmothers (even part-time ones) probably do engage in the traditional socialization behaviors with their stepchildren. This "mothering" means more contact between stepmother and stepchild, and thus the opportunity exists for conflict to occur.

Evidence from a study by psychologists Clingempeel, Ievoli, and Brand (1984) shows that stepmother-stepchild relationships differ depending on the sex of the stepchild. The stepmother-stepdaughter relationship was the least positive of the stepparent-stepchild relationships in this study. When stepdaughters did not perceive love from their stepmothers, stepdaughters scored higher on measures of aggression, lower on measures of inhibition, and lower on measures of self-esteem. Stepmothers who showed positive communication toward the stepdaughter had stepdaughters with higher self-esteem. The quality of the step-mother-stepdaughter relationship was negatively associated with the frequency of visits with the biological mother, a finding not true of step-sons. Other studies support this finding, suggesting that regular contact with the biological mother creates tensions in the stepfamily and com-plicates the children's relations with their stepmothers. One explanation for this finding is that children may find it more difficult to replace mothers than fathers (Furstenberg and Nord, 1985).

We want to end this section with one qualification. When studies report on the difficulties of stepparent-stepchild relationships, these prob-lems concern only a minority of children. For the *majority* of chil-dren in remarriages, major problems with stepparents do not surface or are not reported. Intense emotions and closeness between family members may be less than that found in first families, but trauma and crisis are rare (Duberman, 1975; Ferri, 1984).

Rewards Associated With Stepparenting

The literature rarely reports the benefits associated with the task of parenting someone else's children. If anything, it tends to be discour-aging, focusing on negative effects more than positive outcomes. We believe, however, that benefits are also part of living in a stepfamily.

One such benefit is that the responsibility of child rearing and child care may be shared with another family. When relations between ex-spouses are amicable and flexible, some degree of freedom from full-time parenting is permitted.

Another benefit stems from the (potentially) greater objectivity a step-parent can bring to the parenting process. Because a stepparent is usually not as emotionally attached to, and identified with, a child as is a biological parent he or she can view both the parent's and child's behavior in a more detached way. The stepparent can act as a relatively neutral mediator during times of crisis. This "outsider" perspective also means that the stepparent may gain insights into patterns of parent-child inter-action that remain hidden from the participants themselves. For example, a mother who is too self-effacing with her children may not realize how she is behaving. Her husband who watches the parent-child interaction can help her to realize that if she wants the children's respect she must respect and attend to her own needs as well as to their needs.

A stepparent who befriends a stepchild can also be a more objective sounding board for the child's concerns. For example, a child could ask a stepparent how best to approach his or her parent for something. A stepparent can be a friend, a source of support, and a source of information on subjects children feel uncomfortable discussing with one of his or her biological parents.

A stepparent also has the potential of opening the family to new ideas, different politics, new appreciations for art, music, literature, sports, or other leisure activities. When new stepmembers bring different values and experiences into the family, the family as a group expands its perspectives and opportunities.

Last, but not least, only with remarriage after divorce does a child have an alternative living arrangement that includes a biological parent. In first families, extended kin can sometimes serve as an alternative residence. But only in remarriage following divorce can a child elect to live with a biological parent—a person who was more intimately involved with their life from the beginning.

In summary, the studies that examine stepfather and stepmother difficulties generally find that stepfathers feel less secure about their parenting than is justified by the feelings of their wives and stepchildren. Stepfathers on the average are detached from their stepchildren, and both parents and children perceive this detachment. The stepmother role is the least satisfying of all stepfamily roles, according to the literature. The distress of women as stepmothers is mirrored in the sex differences related to children's adjustment to remarriage. Daughters are reported to have more trouble adapting to a parent's remarriage than are sons. Finally, there are benefits that accrue to adults and children who live in stepfamilies that are seldom acknowledged but that help to make life more enriched for stepfamily members.

SIBLING RELATIONSHIPS

When a child's divorced or widowed parent(s) remarry, the kinship network expands, and he or she has the opportunity to develop ongoing relations with a wide variety of steprelatives. We discuss several of these relationships at the end of this chapter. The second closest set of kin relations, after parents, are sibling relationships. We consider in this section how sibling and stepsibling relationships are affected by remarriage.

Stepsiblings

An accurate estimate of the number of children who have step-siblings cannot be determined. This is because there is no accurate way of predicting how many remarried men who have children from a prior marriage marry women with children. One educated guess comes from a longitudinal study conducted in Wisconsin that showed three-quarters of remarried men had children from their first marriage (Sewell and Hauser, 1975). Larry Bumpass (1984) estimates that between 40% and 50% of the children entering remarriages have stepsiblings. Thus although we do not know the exact figure, we can nevertheless conclude that a significant number of children in stepfamilies have step-siblings. We also can surmise with some accuracy that the majority of these stepsibling relationships develop within a "visiting" arrangement, for a stepfather's children usually live in another home with their own biological mother. The visiting situation can change when, for one or more of the reasons discussed earlier, a stepchild changes residence. We reported in Chapter 5 that in as many as 20% of families children move from one parental home to another. When this happens, the dynamics of the stepsibling relationship also change.

Problems in Stepsibling Adjustment

Little empirical information has been gathered on stepsibling relation-ships. One study (Lutz, 1973) of 103 teenagers found that having step-siblings was positively associated with higher stress. Several of the young people in this study wrote comments indicating that they experienced stress under two circumstances: (a) when their parents argued over the children in the family, and (b) when the children and stepchildren in the family were not treated in the same way.

One of us (Ihinger-Tallman, 1985) conducted a small study to learn more about stepsibling relationships. A dozen college students were interviewed about their relationships with siblings and stepsiblings. We report the substance of these interviews below. Remember, however, that these data are only suggestive since the findings refer to only a dozen case studies.

Stepsiblings were generally predisposed to like each other. Good feel-ings prevailed between stepsibs, whether they lived in separate residences or together. The data suggest that if there were feelings of hostility or dislike between children, they generally did not extend across the entire sibling group. Rather, negative feelings were directed toward only one stepsib. When poor relations between children were mentioned, they generally stemmed from differential treatment by parent and step-parent— a common complaint expressed by these young people.

When stepsiblings were close in age and of the same sex, sometimes the differential treatment brought the children closer together. For example, when fifth-grader Michelle (whose quote you read at the beginning of this chapter) moved to her father's house, she began living with Stephanie, a stepsister seven months older than herself. According to Michelle, the girls either fought with each other or ignored each other for the first two years they lived together. Although this wasn't exactly a Cinderella story, it became obvious to both girls during this time that Michelle's stepmother demanded things from her that she did not expect from her own daughter. By the time the two girls were in the seventh grade they were both interested in boys and shared common school experiences. About this time Stephanie began sticking up for Michelle and taking her stepsister's side in disputes when her mother made demands on Michelle, expecting her to do things Stephanie did not have to do. According to Michelle, their common interests and the discriminatory treatment by her stepmother brought them closer together.

One source of strained relations between stepsiblings stems from the observation that their stepsiblings received less strict discipline from their father than was applied to them. Children observed that their step-mother's children were permitted to do and say things that they themselves were punished for, such as making a mess in the house or talking back to adults. Although resentment sometimes accompanied these observations, generally children did not seem to let this interfere with their relationship with each other. Children seemed to understand that their own father had difficulty disciplining someone else's children. If any resentment followed from these observations, it tended to center on the stepparent, not their stepsiblings or their own father.

One problem that clinicians discuss but researchers have not yet studied involves the potential sexual involvement between adolescent stepsiblings. According to family therapist David Baptiste (1986: 5), "the absence of the incest taboo in stepfamilies can lead to the loosening of sexual boundaries, and even to sexual involvement." He suggests that interpersonal conflict and hostility is one way that opposite sex adolescent stepsiblings keep from developing strong feelings of attachment to one another. Remarried parents may interpret the children's conflict as a failure on their part to establish a close family system. They sometimes intensify sexual feelings between stepsiblings by insisting that the teenagers cease and desist the fighting and become friends. Ensuing friendship and closeness, combined with physical attraction, awakens sexual feelings. Some therapists suggest defusing these feelings by acknowledging how hard it must be for young people who could be dating one another to be living in the same house. When the difficulty is uncovered and discussed, teenagers can admit that they feel it is impossible to be like brothers and sisters when there are no blood ties. Thus underlying tensions can be relieved and the conflict can diminish.

Although numerous clinical writers suggest that sexual attraction between stepmembers can be problematic, researchers have not yet examined this contention. One question from our own study asked parents if sexual attraction was ever a problem between the stepmembers in their families. Only 3.8% of the 784 respondents acknowledged that it was (Pasley and Ihinger-Tallman, 1980).

Sibling and Stepsibling Bonding

Sibling socialization is rarely studied. When children in the family are the subject of study, the focus usually turns to the parent-child relationship because parents are recognized as the principle socializers of children. However, brothers and sisters are not simply family members who share an environment. They are also influencial agents of socialization. Through everyday interactions with one another and their reactions to each other's behavior, siblings help develop each other's self-conceptions, or identities. In addition, in most families siblings perform many useful functions for one another. Some of the things siblings do for each other include acting as defenders/protectors (against parents and other siblings as well as persons outside the family), interpreting the outside world for one another, teaching each other about social relationships and social processes such as equity, justice, coalition formation, and how to bargain and negotiate. Siblings are everwatchful, and they regulate each other's behavior; they share information, material goods, and friends (Schvandevelt and Ihinger, 1979).

A few writers have set out to explain the factors responsible for bringing siblings close to one another. They have attempted to identify the situations or behaviors that foster strong bonds between siblings.

Clinicians Stephen Bank and Michael Kahn (1982) suggest that siblings develop strong attachments when parents fail to meet the needs of their children adequately. These authors do not suggest that parents intentionally neglect their children and parent poorly, although in a few cases that may be true. Inadequate parenting more frequently results from circumstances such as divorce, death, long periods of unemployment, illness, and emotional or mental problems. If children are required to depend upon one another for protection or for nurturance during such family crises, they likely develop strong attachments. Elinor Rosenberg (1980) concurs with this assessment. She adds that in families where parents are unable to respond to their children's physical and emotional needs, the children naturally gravitate toward each other to achieve this sense of security. This does not mean that children spontaneously and naturally help one another. A crisis situation may result in increased conflict and competition, reflecting a child's individual needs and/or intrapsychic conflict. Thus other factors are necessary for a sense of closeness to develop between siblings. These factors are discussed in a recent article (Ihinger-Tallman, forthcoming). The ideas are summarized as follows.

One family characteristic that is thought to be a necessary contributor to the process of sibling bonding is simply access: Siblings must be available to one another before bonding can occur. Accessibility is fostered by closeness in age and sex, but it can also stem from mutual dependencies. For example, an older sister who takes over some of the "mothering" of her younger brothers/sisters immediately after a parental separation or divorce increases the accessibility between herself and her siblings. She may read them bedtime stories, fix their breakfast, or help with homework. The increased interaction and dependencies that develop on the part of both older and younger siblings increases the closeness between them. Thus with access comes mutual dependency, shared experiences, and potentially rewarding interactions.

Sibling bonding does not necessarily mean that siblings strive to be just like one another. Brothers and sisters may identify with each other and share close feelings, but children also have strong needs to develop their own identity—to be seen as different from their brothers and sisters. Sometimes these needs are so strong that they inhibit attachment and interfere with the development of strong sibling bonds. Another situation inhibiting sibling bonding is when parents or grandparents make negative comparisons between siblings. Whether it is done intentionally or unintentionally, holding the behavior or performance of one child up to a brother or sister can create envy, hostility, or rivalry. Some adults claim they never have outgrown the feelings of jealousy that were created when they were negatively compared to their siblings as children (Ross and Milgram, 1982).

The same factors that foster bonding between siblings likely foster bonding between stepsiblings also. Age and sex similarity, mutually rewarding experiences, mutual dependencies, and shared experiences draw stepsiblings closer to one another. These reflect the benefits of association. However, when the costs of association are perceived to outweigh the benefits, stepsiblings will not develop close relationships. In fact, they may intentionally draw apart. The possible costs are numerous. They include the perception of less time, attention, resources and affection from their own parent or biological siblings because of the presence of stepsiblings. If stepsiblings are forced to share their friends and possessions (rooms, toys, pets), they may feel resentment. Some youngsters have to make very costly adjustments when they and their parent move to the home and neighborhood of a stepparent and stepsiblings. This situation is well illustrated by a quote from a young teenager who, three months after moving with her mother into the home of her new stepfather and stepsiblings complained, "We've had to give up everything, and they haven't even changed the kind of hair conditioner they use."

Two factors in Duberman's (1975) study were found to foster good sibling relations. One was whether the parents themselves had a good relationship. The second was whether the stepparent had a good relationship with the stepchildren. Under these circumstances, stepsiblings were more likely to have a good relationship with each other. Some remarried parents in Duberman's study felt that a child in common (a half-sibling to the other children in the family) brought the children closer together and helped them form closer relations. What are the probabilities of a child getting a half-sibling? We discuss this below.

Half-Siblings

Based upon 1980 census information, Bumpass (1984) estimates that about 66% of the children entering a remarriage are likely to have a stepsibling or to acquire a half-sibling. Only about 16% will have both.

Almost half of the children entering remarriage have mothers who are under the age of 30. That means that the majority of children are young when they begin their family life as members of stepfamilies. According to Bumpass, about 33% are preschoolers, 49% are school age, and only 16% are teenagers (14-17 years old).

Given the relatively young ages of mothers at remarriage, if a half-sibling is born into the stepfamily, it is likely to happen within the first four years of the marriage—80% of new births occur within that time. A total of 11% of the children in remarriage have mothers who are already pregnant at the time of the marriage, and 24% gain a half-sibling within 18 months of the remarriage. Half-sibling births, however, are becoming less frequent. The rate of first births in remarriage declined during the decade of the 1970s, just as the overall fertility rate declined. Thus although increased rates of parental divorce and remarriage brought more children into stepfamilies, fewer of these marriages now include children in common of the remarried partners.

If a child's stepfather was previously married the likelihood of having a half-sibling is lessened. Of stepchildren with a never-married stepfather, 44% had a half-sibling, whereas only 26% with a formerly married stepfather did so.

We know more about the probabilities of having a half-sibling than we do about the nature of relationships between half-siblings. As mentioned earlier, Duberman's (1975) study explored this issue. In that report parents concluded that the birth of a new baby in the family helped the stepsiblings who were already in the family to develop deeper attachments.

To summarize, stepsiblings are predisposed to like one another, all else being equal. This is because of the normative pressure that exists in our society for family members to hold affectionate feelings for one another (Adams, 1968). Due to the lack of any different norms for step kin, this general societal expectation of affection is assumed to hold for stepsiblings. And children themselves report generally positive feelings toward stepsiblings. When siblings are close in age and share common experiences, when they develop mutual dependencies upon one another, and when the costs of association are relatively equal, then stepsiblings are expected to develop a close attachment. There is little evidence that tells of the impact on the other children in the family when a half-sibling is born to a stepfamily or of the relationships that develop between half-siblings.

EXTENDED KIN TIES AND FRIENDS

Death and divorce disrupts the living arrangements and lifestyle of all family members. Not only are the relationships of the nuclear family disrupted and changed, but relatives (kin), friendship, and community ties are disrupted as well. Studies of adjustment after divorce show that the loss of social support can be one of the most difficult problems facing a single parent. Although ties with own kin usually do not suffer, contact with ex-spouse's kin, friends, and group participation (such as clubs and volunteer organizations) drops off (Spicer and Hampe, 1975; Renne, 1971). Remarriage, on the other hand, offers new opportunities for interaction and support and gives family members the chance to develop relations with a variety of new step kin. As noted earlier, remarriage may enrich the kinship network for children as well as provide a larger pool of relatives from which loving and nurturing relationships can develop. Sharing children among a greater number of people who become "family" through divorce and remarriage is one way children can be "shared," thus compensating for a declining fertility rate (Furstenberg, 1981; Riley, 1982).

There are few empirical studies from which to draw conclusions about the quality and quantity of kin relationships after remarriage. We present in this section the evidence that is available.

Relations with Grandparents

Children are often supported through the emotional experience of divorce and remarriage by relatives outside the nuclear family. Grandparents can be one source of stability for children. The extent of support offered often depends on which parent the grandparent is related to. Divorce can weaken the ties to a child's father's relatives when, as is usually the case, the child remains in the care of his or her mother. However, separation from paternal grandparents is less likely if a father maintains close contact with his child after a divorce (Anspach, 1976; Spicer and Hampe, 1975). Much of what we know about stepgrandparent relations comes from two studies by Furstenberg and his colleagues. These studies are the source of the information provided here.

Many mothers do attempt to maintain contact with their ex-in-laws, if only for the sake of the children. They sometimes go to considerable trouble to arrange weekend or vacation visits. Remarried parents have generally felt that it was "in the child's best interests not to destroy kinship connections that might be emotionally and materially important to their offspring" (Furstenberg and Spanier, 1984: 128). Even when the divorced spouses do not get along, they usually acknowledge the rights of the grandparents to see the children. Most children continue to see their grandparents occasionally throughout the year. Between 67% and 75% of the children in Furstenberg and Spanier's Pennsylvania study (1984) visited the parents of their nonresidential parent a few times a year or more; 33% saw them at least once or twice a month.

When parents remarry, their own parents (the children's stepgrand-parents) usually accept the children into the family. In the National Survey of Children three-quarters of the remarried respondents reported no difficulty with the older generation accepting the new stepgrand-children. Associated with the acceptance on the part of the older generation is the encouragement of children to adopt kinship terms ("grandpa," "poppa," and so on) for these new relatives. Furstenberg and Spanier (1984) suggest that kin relations after remarriage are analagous to an accordian that expands rather than a pie that must be divided up into ever smaller pieces.

A desire on the part of the older generation to strengthen the bonds with their own adult children has been suggested as a motive for the acceptance of a new in-law and stepgrandchildren. This may be a valid way to maintain kinship bonds. Ties to remarrying children may be endangered if parents treat the new son- or daughter-in-law and his or her children as nonfamily (Furstenberg and Spanier, 1984).

Relations with Friends

Friendships are affected by divorce and remarriage, too. Only 50% of the women in one study of divorce reported that they kept their old friends through the period of separation and divorce. Friends evidently find it difficult to be loyal to both partners of the divorce (Goode, 1965). Yet, friends provide critical emotional support to divorced partners during a time of personal distress.

A recent study of friendship by Rubin (1985) reports that when a married couple's divorced friend is unhappy, a continuing friendship with that person affirms their marriage. It reminds them that whatever their problems, married life is better than being single. When divorced friends are happy, however, it's another matter. Then the friendship heightens the ambivalence in the married couple's life and internal conflict results.

Another writer who studied separation and divorce writes, "In one way or another separation is a period in which friendships are dissolved and new ones are formed" (Halem, 1982: 151). A total of 42% of

Lynne Halem's (1982) sample of divorced men and 63% of the women reported that meeting new people of the same or opposite sex was one of the more difficult problems associated with separation.

No studies to our knowledge have examined what happens to friendships after remarriage. We could speculate that since the remarried situation is not a crisis, no cataclysmic changes with regard to friendships occur. With ordinary life changes, the people with whom remarried people interact shift and change accordingly as the couple's or family's needs change. This is the same process that happens with friendships in first marriages.

Somewhat related to this issue is the unpublished finding from our study of remarrieds that asked about friend's and relative's support of the couples' remarriage. We found that 34% of our respondents felt that friends and kin were "extremely supportive" of the new union. Only 10% felt few or none were supportive.

In summary, the extent to which remarried couples integrate kin and friends into their family life is only beginning to be understood. We know these relationships are sources of support and affection for persons who separate and/or divorce. After remarriage, the majority of those in the older generation continue to extend support and affection toward new in-laws and stepgrandchildren. We know much less about friendship and how it is affected by marital dissolution and remarriage. The evidence that exists hints that a good number of the friendships held prior to a divorce will terminate.

DISCUSSION QUESTIONS

(1) What might be done to enhance the quality of stepparent-stepchild relationships?
(2) Are there other possible explanations for the less positive interactions between stepmothers and stepdaughters than the ones offered in this chapter?
(3) How might you explain the differences between stepmother and stepdaughter and stepmother and stepson relationships?
(4) What might spouses do to foster closeness between siblings? How might this be different depending on the children's ages?
(5) What kinds of interactions between stepfamily members and extended kin can enrich the relationship?

RELATED READINGS

FURSTENBERG, F. F., Jr., and G. SPANIER (1984) Recycling the Family: Remarriage After Divorce. Beverly Hills, CA: Sage.

IHINGER-TALLMAN, M. (forthcoming) "Sibling and stepsibling bonding in stepfamilies," in Remarriage and Stepparenting Today: Research and Theory. Beverly Hills, CA: Sage.

VISHER, E. B. and J. S. VISHER (1982) How to Win as a Stepparent. New York: Brunner/Mazel.

Helping Remarrieds Make It

HABITATION

Marriage is not
a house or even a tent

it is before that, and colder:

the edge of the forest, the edge
of the desert
the unpainted stairs
at the back where we squat
outside, eating popcorn

the edge of the receding glacier

where painfully and with wonder
at having survived even
this far

we are learning to make fire

—Margaret Atwood, *Selected Poems,*
Simon and Schuster, 1976. Reprinted
by permission of the author.

THE PREVIOUS CHAPTERS of this volume have explored the complexities of remarriage and highlighted the problems that contribute to an almost 60% redivorce rate. However, looking at the redivorce rate from another perspective means that 40% of remarriages remain intact over time. In this chapter we consider the factors that contribute to this stability and describe how couples can be helped to develop stable marital relationships. Specifically, we summarize two perspectives that describe the process of stepfamily development. These perspectives were conceptualized by family therapists from their work with remarried couples. We also identify and describe the informal and formal ways members of remarried families can gain and use information to enhance their family life. Finally, we explore some of the public policy issues that relate to remarriage.

Much of the advice offered members of remarried families stems from the experiences of therapists and other helping professionals in clinical settings. It does not usually stem from empirical sources. Thus a primary limitation of this clinical information is that it is based on insights gained from working with persons who are experiencing more stress than is probably found in the general population. In other words, those in therapy are likely not to be representative of the broader population of remarried spouses.

At the same time, some conceptualizations of stepfamily adjustment derived from these clinical settings are adaptable and useful for all stepfamilies. We summarize the ideas from two of these frameworks developed by David Mills (1984) and Patricia Papernow (1984).

MODELS OF STEPFAMILY ADJUSTMENT

The models of Mills and Papernow each have distinct ideas, but common themes are also evident in them. In both, adjustment and integration result from (1) "giving up the dream" or fantasies and unrealistic expectations members hold for the new family, (2) gaining clarity about the feelings and needs of individual family members, and (3) creating a new commitment to develop roles, rules, and routines of living together as a unit.

Several tasks are required as remarried family members attempt to resolve the issues that move them from giving up the dream to creating new commitments. Feelings of loss and grief accompany not only the termination of the first family, but are commonly experienced in the formation of a new family. Expecting and hoping for something that is not realized is a painful experience. For example, a woman who marries and thinks or hopes her new husband will be a kind, caring male role model for her son experiences disappointment when reality is characterized by open, hostile conflict between the two. Part of giving up the dream is also having the courage and stamina to not give up too quickly the belief that the family can make it.

Although giving up one's dreams are painful, the real work of the family is part of the second and third themes, where member's needs and feelings are recognized and incorporated into the "master plan" for the new family. Here, family members must explore possible roles, rules, and rituals as they search for ones that will uniquely fit their particular family. As they determine what these are, the family will likely struggle with trying to clarify issues around power and control in the family. Usually this means that the marital pair must make it clear to the children and stepchildren, as well as former and current kin, that they will assume responsibility for directing the activities of the family unit, that they alone will determine if and when the family will end.

The models of Papernow and Mills also suggest several general strategies that assist in moving members through these tasks. For example, gaining information about the realities of stepfamily life can be most helpful. This information can be particularly helpful early in the remarriage when members are confronted with the disillusionment of unrealized dreams. Information can aid members in understanding that many of the issues they face are common to many, if not most, stepfamilies. The ability to identify individual and family goals, as well as devise a plan for meeting these goals, can provide the family with a sense of common direction, as well as experiences that promote the identification of feelings and effective communication patterns. Daily life can often be enhanced by stepparents adopting certain strategies for setting limits and solving the daily problems that arise. For if the problems remain unresolved, time can diminish the positive regard between family members (Mills, 1984; Stern, 1978).

POPULAR ADVICE, EDUCATIONAL STRATEGIES, AND THERAPEUTIC INTERVENTION

Although the models of stepfamily adjustment discussed earlier lend themselves to the use of certain specific strategies, other sources of assistance to remarried families are also available. Three sources will be discussed.

Informal Help-seeking

The primary purpose of informal help-seeking strategies is to normalize the experience of remarried families. Not unlike first-time parents, stepfamilies have few means for assessing whether their experience is unique or common to stepfamily living in general. Stepfamily members are advised by most "experts" to learn early that families come in a variety of forms—not just the first-married ideal.

The availability of self-help books increases annually. Many of these books take a case-study approach wherein a stepparent shares his or her personal experience with the reader. Others are written by therapists or persons in various helping professions. Coleman, Ganong, and Gringrich (1985) report that nearly half of the self-help books they examined were written by authors who were themselves stepparents. They offer guidelines for handling the problems that are common to stepfamilies based on their personal experiences.

Not only are the number of popular books increasing, but the topics of remarriage and stepparenting are receiving more attention in the popular press, especially newspaper and magazine articles. Three groups of researchers have recently conducted a content analysis of the lay literature to discern the trends and content of this literature. We (Pasley and Ihinger-Tallman, 1985) reviewed 119 articles published in popular magazines between 1940 and 1980 (this number represented the totality of articles published during that time). We found an increase in the number of articles published, as well as an increase in the number of "factual" articles. We also found the lay literature to be more optimistic in its overall tone, and it often implied more simplistic solutions to complex problems than was evident in the professional literature. Of the numerous topics discussed in the articles we reviewed, issues related to the stepparent-stepchild relationship were most prominent. We concluded that the increasing availability of articles in the lay literature can assist the "normalization" of stepfamily experiences since these publications appeal to a broader audience than does the professional literature.

Laurel Lagoni and Alicia Skinner Cook (1985) conducted a content analysis of five popular magazines, examining 30 articles. Although they found no significant increase in the number of articles on stepfamilies published by these magazines during the years 1961-1982, they did determine that the content of the articles focused on the needs of children and the ambiguity of the stepparent role. On the other hand, the issues of finance and legalities received little attention. As mentioned earlier, we also found the stepparent-stepchild relationship was a primary focus of the articles we investigated (Pasley and Ihinger-Tallman, 1985).

A third study examined the popular literature for expressions of stepfamily strengths (Coleman et al., 1985). Here the authors performed a content analysis of 44 self-help books, 46 magazine articles, and 153 adolescent fiction books. Although in all three bodies of literature some potential strengths were discussed, a common focus of the articles/stories was on the problems of stepfamily life. The authors expressed concern that "the problem orientation may reinforce the negative stereotypes with which stepfamilies must contend, and stepparents may become discouraged, feeling that they are battling against overwhelming odds" (p. 587).

Educational Strategies

Many writers suggest the value of a premarriage educational experience. Such experience can include attending a one-hour lecture on the subject of remarriage/stepparenting, a day-long workshop, or a series of seminars. Often these programs attempt to introduce people to some of the typical experiences that are likely to be encountered in stepfamilies, so that more realistic expectations develop. As a form of *anticipatory socialization* (fantasizing about, experimenting with, rehearsing, or preparing for a role before it is actually assumed), these educational programs can (a) prepare adults and children for the emotional experiences that accompany remarriage and stepfamily life, (b) sensitize them to effective communication skills, and (c) examine the variety of ways remarrieds cope with adjustment stress. Workshop topics have focused on disseminating information about the possible problems inherent in forming a stepfamily. Sometimes they discuss the loss of autonomy, the grieving process, financial and legal considerations, and ways of dealing with the claims of prior places, memories, friends, and child(ren) from a first marriage (Williams and O'Hern, 1979).

There has been an increase in the number of commercially produced guidebooks available to facilitators of educational programs. Three of the more popular educational guides produced commercially are as follows:

CURRIER, C. (1982) Learning to Step Together. Boston, MA: Stepfamily Association of America.

LARSON, J. H. and J. D. ANDERSON (1984) Effective Stepparenting. New York: Family Service Association of America.

ALBERT, L. and E. EINSTEIN (1986) Strengthening Stepfamilies. Circle Pines, MN: American Guidance Service.

Some limited research has attempted to assess the value of participation in educational programs. Findings suggest that several positive outcomes come from participation in such programs. Couples develop more realistic expectations for stepfamily living, their conflict is reduced, and role clarity is increased (Brady and Ambler, 1982; Messinger et al., 1978).

Therapeutic Intervention

Most remarried couples do not initially seek out assistance from family therapists, counselors, psychologists or psychiatrists. Instead they commonly wait until problems get out of hand and become so magnified that other options, such as educational programs, are no longer feasible.

For most couples this means that months and perhaps years have passed with members experiencing increasing discomfort. A point is reached when life becomes too painful and the thought of redivorce is seen as a viable option. This is the point when many seek professional help.

Often only one member of the family seeks therapy. Those therapists who specialize in work with stepfamilies comment that it is commonly the stepmother whom they first see (Moynihan-Bradt, personal communication, April 13, 1986; E. B. Visher, personal communication, September 19, 1986). If the client is the stepmother, she often seeks help to test the validity of her perceptions of the situation and to relieve her sense of confusion. Much of what a therapist can offer the client at this time is assurance that what she or he is experiencing is not "all in their head," a fear that is typical of stepmembers who perceive trouble.

Sometimes it is the child who is identified as the client (Baptiste, 1983; Goldberg, 1982). If the client is a child, therapists usually recommend that the entire family be involved in therapy since the acting-out behavior may stem from difficulties within the broader family system (including grandparents and quasi kin).

The clinical literature is full of suggestions for assisting stepfamily adjustment. In reviewing this literature, several common suggestions are apparent. Therapists are encouraged to:

- provide an arena for the resolution of grief resulting from the dissolution of the first marriage;
- give spouses permission to consider their needs as equal to the needs of children;
- assist family members to develop problem-solving and negotiation skills;
- provide an environment where alternative ways of dealing with the complexity of the two households of the binuclear family can be explored;
- identify stepparenting behaviors that enhance the relationship between stepparent and stepchild;
- explore alternative roles, rules, and rituals; and
- consolidate parental authority.

Clinical writers concur that therapists must consider whom to include in the therapy sessions, what the presenting problems are, and which subgroups in the family appear to be affected most (Sager et al., 1980; Visher and Visher, forthcoming). In part, these considerations will depend on the stage of stepfamily development the therapists perceive the clients to be in. Papernow (1984), a therapist and researcher, has identified seven stages of stepfamily development. She suggests that a therapist will not likely be sought out in *Stage 1—Fantasy*—where the adults expect instant love and adjustment. In this stage the children may try to ignore the stepparent in hopes that he or she will go away and the biological parents will reunite. Typically stepfamilies may participate in some type of educational program in this stage, but therapy is not yet a viable alternative. Stepfamilies experiencing *Stage 2—Assimilation*—are not likely to seek out professional help. Here they attempt to realize their fantasies, yet get a vague sense that things are not right. *Stage 3—Awareness*—typically finds a member of the stepfamily initiating contact with a therapist. Although the subgroups in the family are divided along biological lines, spouses are aware of the need for change if the family is to continue. *Stages 4 and 5—Mobilization and Action*—is a time when strong emotions are expressed and conflict is typically most intense. Often the stepparent with no children of his or her own is excluded from the biological subgroup. This is followed by a period where the couple begins working together to find solutions and clarify boundaries. This is the stage when Emily and John Visher (in press), two family therapists, suggest that extended kin and quasi kin be involved in counseling. Final *Stages 6 and 7—Contact and Resolution*—involve the spouses working well together. Bonding occurs between stepparent and stepchild during these stages. In part, this results from the clarity that develops in the stepparent role and the ability of the stepfamily to deal more effectively with quasi kin.

Fishman and Hamel (1981) caution counselors not to assume stepfamily life is a replica of first families. If differences are not recognized, then alternative roles and rules that "fit" a particular stepfamily will not have the opportunity to develop. Baptiste (1984) cautions that therapists separate stepfamily issues from issues that result from cultural and racial variations within a family. That is, a Hispanic husband may expect certain behaviors from his Anglo wife that stem from his cultural heritage and have no connection to the fact that she is the residential stepmother to his children.

Other authors have offered examples of therapeutic intervention for specific groups of professionals. For example, we (Pasley and Ihinger-Tallman, 1986) have offered suggestions for counselors who work in school systems. Coleman et al. (1984) offer suggestions for teachers working with children living in stepfamilies—teachers who are often called upon to provide informal counseling to students in need of help. These authors suggest that teachers take care not to *assume* that a stepchild will have problems, nor should they make assumptions about the nature of the child's home life. Teachers have the opportunity to promote activities that do not put stepchildren in awkward positions. They can help children to see the positive aspects of stepfamily life, including: (1) greater flexibility, (2) multiple role models, (3) extended kin network, (4) a higher standard of living, (5) happy parents, and (6) additional siblings.

Although one-on-one therapeutic interventions may meet the needs of some stepfamilies, group therapeutic interventions meet the needs of others. Couple groups are suggested when several problem sources need to be addressed: lack of consolidation of the couple, unresolved mourning of lost relationships, and guilt and conflict about children (Cohn et al., 1982). Group experiences provide the couple with time away from the children to work on issues with the support of others who are in the same situation, and who are likely struggling with some of the same problems. In fact, when a couple seems "stuck" in couple or family therapy, a change to group sessions can assist them in breaking through to new insights. Further, support groups may be helpful in providing families with a sense of shared experience and the opportunity to consider a wider variety of solutions to common problems. Discussion of the personal experiences of participants can offer support to individual members so that they realize their experiences and perceptions are shared by others. This knowledge may increase their self-confidence and sense of control over the situation.

In summary, at least three general types of help are available to remarried couples. *Informal techniques* principally involve lay literature written in a self-help format. *Educational strategies* involve information-giving programs, and *therapeutic intervention techniques* involve counseling sessions. Therapeutic strategies are used often when the problems confronting the stepfamily are too serious for other strategies to be of help. Some literature is available for school personnel who counsel children in stepfamilies when difficulties at home cause behavior or learning problems in school. Support groups are another source of help to remarried couples who need or want to interact with others facing similar problems. We have very little empirical evidence that assesses the value of these strategies and intervention techniques for enhancing stepfamily life.

THE BROADER PICTURE: POLICY ISSUES

The problems of remarriage are not only problems for remarried individuals; their problems become social problems. Remarriage results from a high divorce rate, and this rate has been linked to the rapid social change occurring in the United States during the past century. The accumulation of these changes affects the family's role in society. In many ways, as implied throughout this book, we are experiencing a "cultural lag"—a situation wherein family behavior, and some laws related to the family (divorce, custody), have changed but attitudes and values about family life have lagged behind. We have established that divorce and remarriage are a frequent occurrence today. Yet, in the United States we maintain the values and norms that support single, life-long marriages. As a consequence, the attitude is conveyed that remarried families are fundamentally troubled or even pathological. Indeed, the sources of the problems faced by remarried families may lie more in the lack of societal support than in personal pathology.

At the government level, legislatures and court systems have tried to stay away from implementing policy directly to family behavior. When family policy has been formulated, care has been taken to put limits on services. Additionally, services that are directed to families are presented in such a way as to designate the receiving families as "special" or "deviant." This is because the state is "likely to be charged with trespassing upon cherished areas of privacy" if there is a strong attempt to regulate behavior that is within the family's domain (Parker, 1982: 358). Policy related to health care, housing, or the welfare of children is aimed at assisting families that in some way have fallen short of self-support.

We cannot begin to present in detail the many complex ways that local, state, and national policy affects remarried families. However, we will describe briefly some ways that schools, the community, and the legal system do influence remarried family life.

Public Schools

Increasingly, school personnel are finding that they must deal with the complex living situations of children in binuclear families. However, they are not usually prepared to deal with these complexities. For example, there is no uniform policy adopted by school districts specifying that: (1) the full range of family information be collected for children (including the names and addresses of residential parent/stepparent and nonresidential parent/stepparent); (2) the school obtain permission to notify both sets of parents about school events involving their common child(ren)'s progress; and (3) a standard interpretation of "custody" be adopted so that there is a common understanding of just who has access to the child.

There are many reasons for this lack of a systematic policy. The school is placed in a vulnerable position when divorced parents do not have cordial relations with one another. Ill feelings about giving information to the "other" parent are vented against school personnel. Other reasons include the complex legal issues surrounding custody; the reluctance of school personnel to invade a family's privacy; budget and time constraints that do not always permit two parent-teacher conferences, two report cards, and so on; and finally, the desire for equal treatment of children's parent-school relations gets interpreted as treating every home according to the "first-married" model (Ricci, 1980). Thus it is left to individual parents to inform their child's school personnel about what they personally need and want. Generally, if all adults in the binuclear family make clear that their concern is the welfare of the child and his or her education, the school will adapt its policy to meet those concerns.

Community Support

There is a growing awareness of the problems faced by some remarried families, and many educational and counseling programs are being developed to help those who live in binuclear family systems. Communities are becoming increasingly aware of the need for such support. One way they have come to the aid of remarrieds seeking help is to provide educational programs. These programs are offered through religious, educational, civic, mental health, or social welfare organizations.

A growing number of these programs are developed with one of two purposes in mind. One purpose is to assist persons who plan to remarry—or who already have remarried—to better understand their legal and personal obligations to the persons involved in the new family, particularly stepchildren. A second goal is to prevent marriage breakdown through preventive planning. Because there are no clearly defined norms, roles, and beliefs surrounding remarriage (that is, no institutionalized ways of behaving) educating for remarriage is difficult. But efforts are being made.

Legal Issues in Remarriage

There are no special provisions in the American legal system for second and subsequent marriages: For adults, the legal obligations for remarriage are the same as a first marriage. However, additional obligations are undertaken by remarried adults when the marriage creates the status of stepparent and stepchild. Moreover, these obligations are ill-defined and are sources of potential conflict in remarriage (Kargman, 1969). The general rule is that unless a stepchild is adopted by his or her stepparent, the stepparent has no duty to support the child (although some states, such as California, may make the stepparent pay child support for his or her stepchild). This rule stems from common law in which a stepparent is not bound to support a stepchild. As of 1978, only Nebraska had imposed the same statutory civil and criminal liability on stepparents for support of their unadopted stepchildren that it imposes on natural parents (Goldsmith, 1978). Nine other states have altered their legal doctrine with regard to stepparent's duty to support stepchildren who are living with them, a doctrine called *in loco parentis*. In loco parentis exists when the stepparent takes the child into his or her home, acknowledges the child as his or hers, and supports it (Goldsmith, 1978).

The complexity of many legal situations increases when step-relationships are involved. We list only a few in order to illustrate the possible legal entanglements associated with remarriage. *Wrongful death* statutes generally do not give stepchildren the right to recover damages for the death of a stepparent. The step relationship has generally been treated favorably by statutes controlling *insurance* benefits, where an in loco parentis relationship is typically the determining factor in allowing recovery of benefits. Similarly, *worker's compensation* generally honors stepchildren as dependents, although there has been some disparity in court rulings. Some courts have ruled that stepchildren are entitled to *Social Security Insurance* benefits. It is a source of some controversy whether the income of a stepparent should be computed when determining the amount of *welfare assistance* to be granted to a stepchild. States are not uniform in their welfare statutes. Laws of *inheritance* also differ across the 50 states and are probably the most remiss in dealing with the stepparent-stepchild relationship. Bernard Berkowitz writes, "Under testate law, the term 'children' has been held not to include stepchildren absent any clear intent to the contrary" (Berkowitz, 1970: 223).

We conclude this discussion of legal issues by noting that there is little consistency countrywide regarding family law; each individual state develops its own legal doctrine and policy.

CONCLUSIONS

It is possible that the rapid rise in divorce and remarriage evidenced over the past 25 years is leveling off. However, the stepfamily of today likely will not become less common—it is here to stay, with all of its social and interpersonal complications. Yet we are only now beginning to understand the nature of stepfamily life.

The changes in our family system have occurred so rapidly that it is not surprising that social scientists, therapists, educators, and policy-makers seem to be scurrying about trying to put together a comprehensive picture of what we are experiencing—and looking for ways to make that experience positive. Change implies disorganization. Those who are in the business of chronicling this change are in the midst of this disorganization. Thus it is difficult for even the chroniclers to provide a clear picture. The research reported in this book conveys the idea that the first step has been taken. The groundwork is laid for understanding, and the central problems have been identified. The solutions may be harder to come by, for they require value changes, time, and greater commitment of what are already scarce resources. We are encouraged, however, by the way things seem to be proceeding, and we have a good idea of what needs to be done.

DISCUSSION QUESTIONS

(1) How might families best use popular literature to learn about stepfamily issues?

(2) Knowing the major issues facing remarried families, what content should be included in educational programs?

(3) What kinds of things might be done in community settings (schools, doctor's offices) to "normalize" the remarriage experience for children?

(4) Assuming therapists need special training to work effectively with stepfamilies, what information should we be sure they receive?

RELATED READINGS

HANSEN, J. C. and L. MESSINGER (1982) Therapy with Remarried Families. Rockville, MD: Aspren.

See the children and adolescent fiction sources in the bibliography of COLEMAN, M., L. GANONG, and R. GRINGRICH (1985) "Stepfamily strengths: a review of popular literature." Family Relations 34: 583-589.

LUTZ, P. E., E. E. JACOBS, and R. L. MASSON (1981) "Stepfamily counseling: issues and guidelines." School Counselor 29: 189-194.

PASLEY, K. and M. IHINGER-TALLMAN (1986) "Stepfamilies: new challenges for the schools," (pp. 70-111) in T. Fairchild (ed.) Crisis Intervention Strategies for School-Based Helpers. Springfield, IL: Charles C Thomas.

CHAPTER
8

The Challenges for Researchers

We've only just begun...
Before the rising sun
We fly
So many roads to choose
We start out walking and learn to run

INTEREST IN THE study of remarriage and stepparenting has grown during the past decade. Not only have these topics received greater attention by research scholars and clinicians, but the popular press has published books and articles on them, too. There has been a steady increase in the number of articles appearing in the lay literature since 1940 (Pasley and Ihinger-Tallman, 1985).

The problems that face those who research remarriage and stepparenting are the same as for those who study the family field in general. However, investigators of remarriage face some additional problems that limit both the quantity and quality of research. The difficulties of conducting research on remarriage will be discussed in this chapter, as well as the ways that have been devised to overcome them. We also identify the theoretical limitations associated with the study of remarriage.

PROBLEMS IN STUDYING REMARRIAGE

If you were to look closely at the studies of remarriage and stepparenting, some common failures appear. These include:

(1) a failure to use theory in formulating research questions and designing studies;
(2) a failure to explain and interpret findings instead of merely "reporting" results;
(3) the use of poor sampling techniques;
(4) information used is obtained from only one member of the family;
(5) research designs are overly dependent on self-report measures;
(6) assessment is made at only one point in time; and
(7) inappropriate groups are used for comparison.

These characteristics emphasize the primary difficulties that plague the investigation of remarriage and stepfamilies. They are discussed in detail below.

Lack of Theoretical or Conceptual Frameworks

A review of 38 empirical studies on the effects of remarriage on children found that most of the studies lack any theoretical foundation. When comparing the empirical literature with clinically based literature, however, Ganong and Coleman (1986) did find that clinicians incorporated theory as the foundation for their investigation more often than empirical researchers.

The purpose of theory is to explain something about a particular subject. Ideally, theory is abstract, is not time or place bound, has good predictability, and leads to a clearer understanding of the phenomena under study. When a theory is formulated, the propositions of the theory are stated and then tested to determine the accuracy of the conceptualization. This process of conceptualization-testing-reconceptualization is at the heart of the scientific endeavor. However, deriving and testing theory is usually circumvented in studies of remarriage and stepfamily life. Most studies are descriptive in nature; that is, they describe the situations or conditions of remarrieds. They tell "what," but not "how" or "why." In part, the failure of researchers to incorporate theory in their studies has resulted in an implied assumption, labeled the "deficit family" or the "deficit comparison" model (Marotz-Baden et al., 1979).

In a decade review of the research on divorce, desertion, and remarriage, Sharon Price-Bonham and Jack Balswick (1980) made several theoretical recommendations. They emphasized that general systems theory is most useful for conceptualizing both divorce and remarriage. Systems theory principles are able to account for the changes in the family system following divorce, and the influence of extended kin on the remarried family system. Other conceptual approaches also have been used to explain reactions to divorce and adjustment in remarriage: exchange, stress, crisis, and role theories are the most popular. In this text we cannot go into detail about how these theories relate to the study of remarriage. However, we can give a short example of how role theory might be applied to help explain stepfamily relationships.

"Role" theory is in actuality a body of knowledge based on concepts and principles that are more loosely termed *a perspective,* that is, it does not consist of a set of formally stated propositions. Rather, it is a "group of theories, loosely linked networks of hypotheses, isolated constructs about human functioning" (Shaw and Costanzo, 1970: 326). Some of the concepts that cluster within this framework are role expections, role performance, role strain, and role overload. Both structural and interactional aspects of roles have been studied. When social psychologists study role interaction they look at leadership and power relations, conformity, socialization, group and individual decision making, and social learning (Shaw and Costanzo, 1970). So how do scholars interested in remarriage use role theory to guide their thinking and research?

Upon entering a remarriage, stepparents often assume the parental roles of nurturer, provider, and authority figure (traditional components of the parent role). But if this happens before the relationship between the stepchild and stepparent is thoroughly established and characterized by trust and respect (or authority), stepparent's parenting will not be accepted by stepchildren (Fast and Cain, 1966).

Phyllis Stern (1978) found some empirical support for these ideas in her study of stepfather families. She found that a stepfather who assumed the disciplinary role prior to befriending his stepchild did not foster positive stepfamily integration. Giles-Sims (1984a) also used the concepts of role theory (conflicting roles, roles clarity, and role sanctions) to provide greater understanding of the stepparent role. She asked 96 adult members of stepfamilies about their expectations for the involvement of stepparents in child rearing as compared to their feelings about biological parent's involvement. As predicted, she found these adults expected stepparents to be less involved in child rearing than biological parents. However, her participants also reported that they readily accepted this lesser involvement on the part of stepparents.

Clingempeel, Brand, and Segal (forthcoming) integrated the concepts from two other "theories," family development and family ecology, to identify areas of needed research in remarriage and stepparenting. Using Urie Bronfenbrenner's (1979) ideas about contexts of development and interaction, stages of family development, and the findings from recent research studies, these authors offer a series of guidelines for improving the quality of research and identifying lacunae in our current knowledge.

We (Ihinger-Tallman and Pasley, 1981) have developed our own theory that purports to explain the adjustment process in remarried families. We wanted to predict the likelihood of stability in remarriage, hypothesizing that high degrees of commitment, concensus, boundary maintenance, and physical maintenance would be principle influences. We found support for these ideas in an initial test of the theory.

In summary, the majority of studies on remarriage and stepparenting devote little attention to theory as a foundation for the questions asked and the interpretation of findings. Most of them simply describe some aspect of stepfamily life, even though it is theory that helps us to understand remarried family life in a systematic way.

METHODOLOGICAL OBSTACLES

There are a variety of methodological problems encountered when studying remarriage. These involve three of the most important tasks of research: sampling, measurement, and data analysis.

Sampling

One of the most difficult aspects of doing research on remarriage is locating people to study. A primary goal of sampling is to identify a group of potential subjects who are representative of the entire population. In the study of remarriage, it is essential to know what the remarried/stepfamily population looks like. The U.S. Census Bureau has helped in this respect. Current statistics are available from the U.S. Census Bureau that describe basic characteristics of the remarried population, especially those who remarry following divorce. The figures are less precise when we focus on remarriages involving children. Because over 60% of all remarriages involve children, the presence of children in a remarriage becomes an important dimension to study. We have learned a great deal about stepfamilies who have stepchildren living in the home (see Bumpass, 1984). However, even the Census Bureau fails to ask remarried couples if they have nonresidential children, and hence we know very little about this group of stepfamilies.

When there is little information about a particular population, it is difficult for researchers to determine whether the sample they have drawn for a study is "representative" (similar to that population). Without representativeness, researchers cannot legitimately generalize their findings to the broader population, and must be cautious when discussing those findings.

The sample used in a particular study affects the quality of research. Most studies on remarriage use small, self-selected, convenience samples. This has resulted in a body of knowledge based primarily on white, middle-class participants. There are a variety of reasons for this type of sampling: (1) recruiting is easier and less costly if subjects are obtained via word of mouth, advertisements, or from students in college classes; (2) public records (such as marriage license applications) that represent a population may not be obtainable, or the public records may not include the information needed (in this case, prior marital history); (3) assessing public records is time constraining; and (4) obtaining a large, representative sample, is too costly for most researchers.

Clinicians Emily and John Visher (1979) call stepfamilies an "invisible" population. To strangers, stepfamilies resemble first-married families (two adults and children), and stepfamilies often foster this image. (See the preface in Duberman, 1975.) A stepfather may introduce himself to his stepchild's teacher as the child's father. The wish to appear as a first family may stem from the negative stereotype attached to the term "step" (Ganong and Coleman, 1984). The adults may see their prior marital experience as a "failure" and the new family as a means for "making good"; they may want to forget that earlier experience. What this means for the researcher is that many potential participants do not wish to be identified as a stepfamily and are not willing to participate in a study.

Studies that have drawn large, random samples of families usually have a comparatively small number of remarried families included. For example, in a study of general mental health, the sample obtained by T. S. Langer and S. T. Michaels (1963) included 1160 adults (20-59 years of age) but only 186 (about 11%) of these adults had been raised or ever resided in a stepfamily. Similarly, Morris Rosenberg (1965) examined the self-esteem and psychosomatic complaints of adolescents, selecting a random sample of 5024 adolescents from the public high schools in New York state. Of these only 262 children resided in stepfamilies (about 5% of the entire sample). These two studies were conducted at a time before the divorce rate began its steep climb. National studies today would likely include a slightly larger percentage of stepfamilies. It is estimated that close to 35% of all children born in the early 1980s may expect to live with a stepparent during a part of their childhood (Glick, 1984).

Small samples make it difficult to investigate the influence of multiple variables when using certain statistical techniques. Each time another variable is added to the analysis (such as length of marriage), fewer cases are available for the designated categories. For example, if a researcher has a sample of 30 remarried couples and one-third are newly remarried, one-third have been remarried for five years, and one-third have been remarried 10 years, there are only 10 couples in each length of marriage category. Adding other variables (such as sex of children, race or social class) would further reduce the number of cases under consideration in any category. Many authors have suggested the need to investigate more variables if we are to gain a thorough understanding of adjustment to remarriage, yet to do so requires larger, more representative samples.

One final sampling issue is the usefulness of comparing first-married individuals, couples, or families with remarried individuals, couples, or families. The comparison of groups is an essential aspect of science. For example, if the parenting styles of people who hold upper-class status are studied, the researcher has no way of interpreting his or her findings unless the parenting styles of other groups of parents are known. Description alone is not very useful.

Researchers have questioned the validity of using first-married families as a comparison group because if you compare the two groups on length of marriage, for example, you will likely have two groups with dissimilar ages of children. Selecting respondents who are in marriages and remarriages of five years duration might result in first-married couples with preschoolers and middle-aged remarried couples with adolescents.

Alternative suggestions for appropriate comparison groups have been suggested. The participants in a study group on remarriage and stepfamilies funded by the Society for Research in Child Development suggested that only remarried couples with children born to that remarriage or those without children be used as the comparison group with first marrieds. Using single-parent households where the number and age of children are the same as those in the stepfamily sample was another suggestion. Here the researchers could be assured that the groups had a similar history of spousal death or divorce and/or time in a single-parent household. There is some concern that the use of the traditional first-married comparison group continues to foster "deficit family" thinking.

The Realities of Sampling

Having spent hours ourselves combing the marriage license applications to identify the population of remarrieds within a particular county, we know firsthand the amount of time and cost involved. Experience demonstrates that thousands of names taken from these records results in locating the current address of about 50% of potential participants. It certainly is less costly to ask for volunteers from a local service organization or a PTA meeting, to put advertisements seeking subjects in newspapers or on the radio, to recruit students enrolled in classes at the local university, or recruit people who go for help or advice from social workers or psychologists. These ways of sampling are called convenience sampling.

Convenience samples usually gather data from white, middle-class respondents. That is because middle-class people are more willing to volunteer to participate in research projects. Evidence suggests a higher remarriage rate among whites than blacks, so we might expect to find more white than black participants in any given study. However, with this issue not just scholars studying remarriage are at fault. Family research in general has been criticized for the failure to actively recruit a sample that would be characteristic of the general population— multiracial and multiclass.

Measurement

A common problem of doing research is determining how to *operationalize* the concepts that are measured. (Operationalization means determining the best way to measure—gather information on—the variable being examined.) This dilemma is also faced by investigators of remarriage and stepparenting. What often happens is that variables are operationalized in different ways in different studies. For example, several studies on the effects of remarriage on children have assessed child achievement. School grades, teacher ratings of child behavior, and achievement test scores have all been used to measure child achievement. Similarly, researchers investigating the influence of remarriage on a child's social well-being have used reports of delinquent behavior, number of delinquent companions, mental or physical health complaints, and the child's report of satisfaction with his or her life. When researchers proport to measure the same concept but choose different behaviors to do so, the findings from one study cannot be readily compared to another. No consistent picture of the situation results.

Other problems result from the use of different types of methodology. The most common type of method used in studies of the family—and remarriage is no exception—gathers data through self-report (interviews and questionnaires). One criticism with self-report studies is that the questions used are typically developed for a particular study—they are questions, or series of questions, that have not been used before nor are they used afterward by other investigators.

Few studies have used observational methods to assess stepfamily behavior, that is, watching family members interact using camera or video, or personally by the researcher. This is a very expensive way to gather data. Some who have used this method have questioned its value, given the cost of videotaping, coding the tapes by trained observers, and/or transcribing the data. Such costs are prohibitive when large samples are gathered, in terms of both time and money. Critics of this method say that behavior varies from one time to another, and the moment caught on tape may not necessarily reflect "typical" family behavior. They also feel that the knowledge that one is being observed may produce unnatural behavior. However, the method is a valued tool, especially when it is used in conjunction with information obtained from other methods.

Data Analysis

Family research has been criticized for its failure to obtain data from more than one family member (Bokemeir and Monroe, 1983). Usually the wife is chosen as the family informant. It can be argued that to understand *family* life, information must be obtained from several family members. More and more researchers today do try to obtain the same information from both spouses, if not from children.

Researchers working with data from multiple sources face the dilemma of deciding exactly how to analyze the data once they are gathered. A variety of alternatives have been suggested. Commonly, discrepancy scores are created by subtracting the score of one spouse from the score of the other. Husband and wife scores are added together, or they are averaged. Each of these techniques has strengths and weaknesses that the researcher must consider.

DIFFERENCES AND SIMILARITIES IN THE CLINICAL AND EMPIRICAL LITERATURES

Some of the contradictory findings reported in the chapters you read result from the differences between the clinical and empirical literatures.

These differences are apparent in the theories used to guide research, the variables studied, and the methods used to gather information. Ganong and Coleman (1986; forthcoming) completed a critical analysis of the findings from empirical and clinical studies that focused on the effects of remarriage on children. They determined that clinicians tend to be more theoretical in their work than are empirical researchers. Clinicians are also more sensitive to the complex nature of remarriage and the processes involved in stepfamily interaction and family adjustment. Clinicians and empirical researchers use different methods to study children in stepfamilies. Empirical researchers tend to use surveys, collecting information from one person only, whereas clinical investigators rely heavily on clinical impressions and case studies. The latter also tend to collect data from several family members. Ganong and Coleman reported that clinicians were more sensitive to the structural variations in remarriage, whereas empirical researchers tend to ignore this complexity. Researchers tend not to differentiate types of stepfamilies, giving the impression that they assume stepmother families function the same as stepfather families.

As might be expected, the conclusions reported in the two literatures are different. The empirical literature suggests there are few differences between stepchildren and children from first families. The clinical literature tends to report that children in stepfamilies are beset by difficulties.

WHAT CAN BE DONE TO ELIMINATE SOME OF THESE PROBLEMS?

Several authors have discussed the variety of ways for improving the quality of research on remarriage and stepparenting (Esses and Campbell, 1984; Ganong and Coleman, 1984). Basically, all concur that longitudinal research (following a group of families over a period of time) is necessary. Only in this way can we come to understand the changes that occur in families as they experience the transition from divorce or death of a spouse/parent to remarriage. Longitudinal research can reveal the factors that foster adaptation at various points in time.

Scholars also agree that larger, random samples are a must for future research. Larger samples permit examination of multiple variables and encourage more definitive statements about the variety of factors that influence remarriage. When large samples are impossible to gather, researchers must be committed to using reliable and valid instruments, ones that are commonly used by other investigators. Then the findings of one study can be compared to those of another.

Finally, we must move beyond looking only at the influence of family structure. Instead we must begin to examine the processes, and mediators of processes, that influence remarried family life.

In spite of the research problems mentioned here, research on remarriage and stepparenting is improving in quality. Researchers are demonstrating greater commitment to the incorporation of theoretical constructs in the development and design of research projects. It is encouraging that a number of studies reported in this textbook show common results, even given the diversity of methods and samples used. The increase of information and the growth of our understanding about remarriage indicates that, like Paul Williams's lyrics at the beginning of this chapter, although we've just begun, and our initial efforts to study remarriage started out with a walk, we're learning to run.

DISCUSSION QUESTIONS

(1) Given the multiple problems researchers of remarriage face, why not just give up the effort?
(2) Why do you think clinicians and the helping professionals come up with different findings than do empirical researchers?

RELATED READINGS

CHILLMAN, C. (1983) "Remarriage and stepfamilies: research results and implications." pp. 147-163. in E. D. Macklin and R. H. Rubin (eds.) Contemporary Families and Alternative Lifestyles. Beverly Hills, CA: Sage.

PASLEY, K. and M. IHINGER-TALLMAN (eds.) (1984) Special issue on remarriage and stepparenting, July issue, Family Relations.

References

ADAMS, B. N. (1968) Kinship in an Urban Setting. Chicago: Markham.

AHRENFELDT v. AHRENFELDT (1840) 1 Hoff Ch. 497. New York.

ALBERT, L. and E. EINSTEIN (1986) Strengthening Stepfamilies. Circle Pines, MN: American Guidance Service.

AHRONS, C. R. (1979) "The binuclear family: two households, one family." Alternative Lifestyles 2: 499-515.

AHRONS, C. R. (1980) "Joint custody arrangements in the post divorce family." Journal of Divorce 3: 189-205.

AHRONS, C. R. (1981) "The binuclear family: two stepfamilies, two houses." Stepfamily Bulletin 1: 5-6.

ANDERSON, T. O. (1982) "The effect of stepfather/stepchild interaction on stepfamily adjustment." Dissertation Abstracts International 43: 1306A.

ANSPACH, D. (1976) "Kinship and divorce." Journal of Marriage and the Family 38: 323-330.

ARIES, P. (1981) "Introduction to Part 1" pp. 27-33 in J. Dupâquier et al. (eds.) Marriage and Remarriage in Populations of the Past. New York: Academic Press.

ASMUNDSSON, R., S. R. BYSIEWICZ, K. M. COWGILL, A. S. DAHL, W. M. HOWARD, S. S. TAYLOR and P. A. WINSHIP (1983) "Life in remarriage families." Presented at the meeting of the American Association for Marriage and Family Therapy, Washington, D.C.

BANK, S. and M. KAHN (1982) The Sibling Bond. New York: Basic Books.

BAPTISTE, D. A. (1984) "Marital and family therapy with racially/culturally intermarried stepfamilies: issues and guidelines." Family Relations 33: 373-380.

BAPTISTE, D. A. (1986) "How parents intensify sexual feelings between stepsiblings." Remarriage 3: 5-6.

BAPTISTE, D. A., Jr. (1983) "Family therapy with reconstituted families: a crisis-induction approach." American Journal of Family Therapy 11: 5-15.

BECKER, G. S., E. M. LANDIS and R. T. MICHAEL (1977) "An economic analysis of marital instability." Journal of Political Economics 85: 1141-1187.

BELLETTINI, A. (1981) "Le remariage dans la ville et dans la campagne de Bologne au dix-neuvième siècle," pp. 259-272 in J. Dupâquier et al. (eds.) Marriage and Remarriage in Populations of the Past. New York: Academic Press.

BERGLER, E. (1948) Divorce Won't Help. New York: Harper & Brothers.

BERKOWITZ, B. J. (1970) "Legal incidence of today's "step" relationship: Cinderella revisited." Family Law Quarterly 4: 209-229.

BERNARD, J. B. (1980) "Afterward." Journal of Family Issues 1: 561-571.

BIDEAU, A. (1980) "A demographic and social analysis of widowhood and remarriage: the example of the Castellany of Thoissey-en-Dombes, 1670-1840." Journal of Family History 5: 28-43.

BISHOP, J. P. (1891) New Commentaries on the Law of Marriage, Divorce, and Separation. Vol. 2, Mass 187, Mass.

BITTERMAN, C. M. (1968) "The multimarriage family." Social Casework 49: 218-221.

BLOOM, B. L. and K. R. KINDLE (1985) "Demographic factors in the continuing relationship between former spouses." Family Relations 34: 375-381.

BOHANNAN, P. (1970) "Divorce chains, households of remarriages, and multiple divorces," in P. Bohannan (ed.) Divorce and After. Garden City, NY: Doubleday.

BOHANNAN, P. and H. YAHRAES (1979) "Stepfathers as parents," pp. 347-362 in E. Corfman (ed.) Families Today: A Research Sampler on Families and Children.

National Institute of Mental Health Science Monograph. Washington, DC: Government Printing Office.

BOKEMEIR, J. and P. Monroe (1983) "Continued reliance on one respondent in family decision-making studies: a content analysis." Journal of Marriage and the Family 45: 645-652.

BOOTH, A. and S. WELCH (1978) "Spousal consensus and its correlates: a reassessment." Journal of Marriage and the Family 40: 23-32.

BOSS, P. and J. GREENBERG (1984) "Family boundary ambiguity: a new variable in family stress theory." Family Process 23: 535-546.

BOWERMAN, C. E. and D. P. IRISH (1962) "Some relationships of stepchildren to their parents." Marriage and Family Living 24: 113-121.

BOWMAN, M. E. and C. R. AHRONS (1985) "Impact of legal custody status on fathers' parenting postdivorce." Journal of Marriage and the Family 47: 481-488.

BRADY, C. A. and J. AMBLER (1982) "Use of group educational techniques with remarried couples." Family Therapy Collections 2: 145-157.

BRAND, E. and G. W. CLINGEMPEEL (1985) "The interdependencies of husband-wife and stepparent-stepchild relationships in stepmother and stepfather families: a multimethod study." Unpublished manuscript, Pennsylvania State University, Harrisburg.

BRONFENBRENNER, W. (1979) The Ecology of Human Development. Cambridge, MA: Harvard University Press.

BUMPASS, L. (1984) "Some characteristics of children's second families." American Journal of Sociology 90: 608-623.

BURGOYNE, J. and D. CLARK (1982) "Reconstituted families," in R. N. Rapport et al. (eds.) Families in Britian. London: Routledge & Kegan Paul.

CABOURDIN, G. (1981) "Le remariage en France sous l'Ancien Régime (seizième-dix-huitième siècles)," (pp. 273-285) in J. Dupaquier (eds.) Marriage and Remarriage in Populations of the Past. New York: Academic Press.

CALHOUN, A. W. (1917) A Social History of the Family, vol 1: Colonial Period. New York: Barnes & Noble.

CARR, L. G. and L. S. WALSH (1983) "The planter's wife: the experience of white women in seventeenth century Maryland," pp. 321-346 in M. Gordon (ed.) The American Family in Social Historical Perspective. New York: St. Martin's.

CARTER, H. and P. C. GLICK (1976) Marriage and Divorce: A Social and Economic Study. Cambridge, MA: Harvard University Press.

CHERLIN, A. (1978) "Remarriage as an incomplete institution." American Journal of Sociology 84: 634-650.

CHERLIN, A. (1981) Marriage, Divorce, Remarriage. Cambridge, MA: Harvard University Press.

CHERLIN, A. and J. McCARTHY (1985) "Remarried couple households: data from the June 1980 Current Population Survey." Journal of Marriage and the Family 47: 23-30.

CHILMAN, C. (1983) "Remarriage and stepfamilies: research results and implications," pp. 147-163 in E. D. Macklin and R. H. Rubin (eds.) Contemporary Families and Alternative Lifestyles. Beverly Hills, CA: Sage.

CLINGEMPEEL, W. S. (1981) "Quasi-kin relationships and marital quality in stepfather families." Journal of Personality and Social Psychology 41: 890-901.

CLINGEMPEEL, W. S., E. BRAND and R. IEVOLI (1984) "Stepparent-stepchild relationships in stepmother and stepfather families: a multimethod study." Family Relations 33: 465-473.

CLINGEMPEEL, W. S., R. IEVOLI, and E. BRAND (1985) "Structural complexity and
the quality of stepfather-stepchild relationships." Family Process 23: 547-560.

CLINGEMPEEL, W. S. and S. SEGAL (1986) "Stepparent-stepchild relationships and
the psychological adjustment of children in stepmother and stepfather families." Child
Development 57: 474-484.

CLINGEMPEEL, W. S., E. BRAND and S. SEGAL (forthcoming) "A multilevel—
multivariable—developmental perspective for future research on stepfamilies," in
K. Pasley and M. Ihinger-Tallman (eds.) Remarriage and Stepparenting Today: Current Theory and Research. New York: Guilford.

COLEMAN, M. and L. GANONG (forthcoming) "The cultural stereotyping of stepfamilies," in K. Pasley and M. Ihinger-Tallman (eds.) Remarriage and Stepparenting
Today: Current Theory and Research. New York: Guilford.

COLEMAN, M., L. H. GANONG and R. GRINGRICH (1985) "Stepfamily strengths:
a review of the popular literature." Family Relations 34: 583-589.

COLEMAN, M., L. GANONG and J. HENRY (1984) "What teachers should know
about stepfamilies." Childhood Education 60: 306-309.

Connecticut Remarriage Research Group (1983) "Life in remarriage families." Presented
at the meeting of the American Association for Marriage and Family Therapy,
Washington, D.C.

CROHN, H., C. J. SAGER, H. BROWN, E. RODSTEIN and L. WALKER (1982)
"A basis for understanding and treating the remarried family, pp. 159-186 in J. C.
Hansen and L. Messinger (eds.) Therapy with Remarriage Families. Rockville,
MD: Aspen.

CROSBIE-BURNETT, M. (1984) "The centrality of the step relationship: a challenge
to family theory and practice." Family Relations 33: 459-463.

CURRIER, C. (1982) Learning to step together: a course for stepfamily adults. Boston,
MA: Stepfamily Association of America.

DAHL, B. B., H. I. McCUBBIN and G. R. LESTER (1976) "War-induced father absence:
comparing the adjustment of children in reunited, non-reunited and reconstituted
families." International Journal of Sociology of the Family 6: 99-108.

DAVIS, N. Z. (1975) Society and Culture in Early Modern France. Palo Alto, CA:
Stanford University Press.

DeMARIS, A. (1984) "A comparison of remarriages with first marriages on satisfaction
in marriage and its relationship to prior cohabitation." Family Relations 33: 443-449.

DEMOS, J. (1970) A Little Commonwealth: Family Life in Plymouth Colony. London:
Oxford University Press.

DERDEYN, A. P. (1976) "Child custody contests in historical perspective." American
Journal of Psychiatry 133: 1369-1376.

DOLAN, E. M. and J. M. LOWEN (1985) "Remarried family: Challenges and
opportunities." Journal of Home Economics 77: 36-41.

DUBERMAN, L. (1975) The Reconstituted Family: A Study of Remarried Couples and
Their Children. Chicago: Nelson-Hall.

DUPÂQUIER, J., E. HÉLIN, P. LASLETT, M. LIVI-BACCI and S. SOGNER [eds.]
(1981) Marriage and Remarriage in Populations of the Past. New York: Academic
Press.

ESSES, L. and R. CAMPBELL (1984) "Challenges of researching the remarried." Family Relations 33: 415-424.

FARBER, B. (1972) Guardian of Virtue: Salem Families in 1800. New York: Basic Books.

FAST, I. and A. C. CAIN (1966) "The stepparent role: potential for disturbances in family functioning." American Journal of Orthopsychiatry 36: 485-491.

FERNANDO, D.F.S. (1981) "Marriage and remarriage in some Asian civilizations," pp. 89-93 in J. Dupâquier et al. (eds.) Marriage and Remarriage in Populations of the Past. New York: Academic Press.

FERRI, E. (1984) Stepchildren: A National Study. Windsor, England: NFER-Nelson.

FISHMAN, B. and B. HAMEL (1981) "From nuclear to stepfamily ideology: a stressful change." Alternative Lifestyles 4: 181-204.

FISHMAN, B. (1983) "The economic behavior of stepfamilies." Family Relations 32: 359-366.

FOX, G. L. (1985) "Noncustodial fathers," pp. 393-415 in S.M.H. Hanson and F. W. Bozette (eds.) Dimensions of Fatherhood, Beverly Hills, CA: Sage.

FOX, V. C. and M. H. QUITT (1980) "Stage VI, spouse loss," pp. 49-61 in V. C. Fox and M. H. Quitt (eds.) Loving, Parenting, and Dying: The Family Cycle in England and America, Past and Present. New York: Psychohistory Press.

FULTON, J. A. (1979) "Parental reports of children's post-divorce adjustment." Journal of Social Issues 35: 126-139.

FURSTENBERG, F. F., Jr. (1981) "Remarriage and intergenerational relations," pp. 115-141 in R. W. Fogel et al. (eds.) Aging: Stability and Change in the Family. New York: Academic Press.

FURSTENBERG, F. F., Jr. (1982) "Child care after divorce and remarriage." Presented at the MacArthur Foundation's Conference on Child Care and Growth Fostering Environments, Chicago.

FURSTENBERG, F. F., Jr. (forthcoming) "The new extended family: The experience of parents and children after remarriage," in K. Pasley, and M. Ihinger-Tallman (eds.) Remarriage and Stepparenting Today: Current Research and Theory. New York: Guilford.

FURSTENBERG, F. F., Jr., and C. W. NORD (1985) "Parenting apart: patterns of childrearing after marital disruption." Journal of Marriage and the Family, 47: 893-904.

FURSTENBERG, F. F., Jr., C. W. NORD, J. L. PETERSON and N. ZILL (1983) "The life course of children of divorce: marital disruption and parental contact. American Sociological Review 48: 656-668.

FURSTENBERG, F. F. Jr., and J. A. SELTZER (1983) "Divorce and child development." Presented at the annual meeting of the American Orthopsychiatric Association, Boston.

FURSTENBERG, F. F. Jr., and G. B. SPANIER (1984) Recycling the Family: Remarriage After Divorce. Beverly Hills, CA: Sage.

GANONG, L. H. and M. COLEMAN (1984) "The effects of remarriage on children: a review of the empirical literature." Family Relations 33: 389-405.

GANONG, L. H. and M. COLEMAN (1986) "A comparison of clinical and empirical literature on children in stepfamilies." Journal of Marriage and the Family 48: 309-318.

GANONG, L. H. and M. COLEMAN (forthcoming) "Effects of parental remarriage on children: an updated comparison of theories, methods, and findings from clinical and empirical research," in K. Pasley and M. Ihinger-Tallman (eds.) Remarriage and Stepparenting Today: Current Theory and Research. New York: Guilford.

GAUNT, Ø. and O. LÖFGREN (1981) Remarriage in the Nordic countries: The cultural and socio-economic background," pp. 49-60 in J. Dupâquier et al. (eds.) Marriage and Remarriage in Populations of the Past. New York: Academic Press.

GILES-SIMS, J. (1984a) "The stepparent role: Expectations, behavior, and sanctions." Journal of Family Issues 5: 116-130.

GILES-SIMS, J. (1984b) "Stepfamily cohesion, expressiveness and conflict by stepfamily outside-parent relationships." Presented at the annual meeting of the National Council on Family Relations, San Francisco.

GILES-SIMS, J. (1985) "Paternal custody and remarriage." Presented at the annual meeting of the National Council on Family Relations, Dallas, TX.

GLENN, N. D. (1981) "The well-being of persons remarried after divorce." Journal of Family Issues 2: 61-75.

GLENN, N. D. and C. N. WEAVER (1977) "The marital happiness of remarried divorced persons." Journal of Marriage and the Family 39: 331-337.

GLENN, N. D. and C. N. WEAVER (1978) "A multivariate, multisurvey study of marital happiness." Journal of Marriage and the Family 40: 269-282.

GLENWICK, D. S. and J. D. MOWEREY (1986) "When parent becomes peer: loss of intergenerational boundaries in single parent families." Family Relations 35: 57-62.

GLICK, P. C. (1984) "Marriage, divorce, and living arrangements." Journal of Family Issues 5: 7-26.

GOETTING, A. (1982) "The six stations of remarriage: developmental tasks of remarriage after divorce." Family Relations 31: 213-222.

GOLDBERG: I. (1982) "Therapy with stepfamilies involved in joint custody." pp. 219-221 in A. S. Gurman (ed.) Questions and Answers in the Practice of Family Therapy, vol. II. New York: Brunner/Mazel.

GOLDSMITH, J. (1980) "Relationships between former spouses: descriptive findings." Journal of Divorce 4: 1-20.

GOLDSMITH, M. A. (1978) "AFDC eligibility and the federal stepparent regulation." Texas Law Review 56: 79-100.

GOODE, W. J. (1965) "Women in Divorce." New York: Free Press.

GOODY, J. (1983) The Development of the Family and Marriage in Europe. New York: Cambridge University Press.

GREIF, G. L. (1985) "Single fathers rearing children." Journal of Marriage and the Family 47: 185-191.

GREIF, G. L. (1986) "Mothers without custody and child support." Family Relations 35: 87-93.

GRIFFITH, J. D. (1980) "Economy, family, and remarriage." Journal of Family Issues 1: 479-496.

GRIFFITH, J. D., H. P. KOO and C. M. SUCHINDRAN (1985) "Childbearing and family in remarriage." Demography 22: 73-88.

GRIGG, S. (1977) "Toward a theory of remarriage: a case study of Newburyport at the beginning of the Nineteenth century." Journal of Interdisciplinary History 8: 183-220.

GUTTENTAG, M. and P. Secord (1983) Too Many Woman: The Sex Ratio Question. Beverly Hills, CA: Sage.

HAFKIN, M. I. (1981) "Association factors for stepfathers integration within the blended family." Dissertation Abstracts International 42: 4578B.

HALEM, L. C. (1982) Separated and Divorced Women. Westport, CT: Greenwood.

HALLIDAY, T. C. (1980) "Remarriage: the more complete institution." American Journal of Sociology 86: 630-635.

HALPERIN, S. M. and T. A. SMITH (1983) "Differences in stepchildren's perceptions of their stepfathers and natural fathers: implications for family therapy." Journal of Divorce 7: 19-30.

HANNA, S. L. and P. K. KNAUB (1981) "Cohabitation before remarriage: its relationships to family strengths." Alternative Lifestyles 4: 507-522.

HANSEN, H. O. (1981) "The importance of remarriage in traditional and modern societies: Ireland during the eighteenth and nineteenth centuries, and the cohort of Danish women born between 1926 and 1935," pp. 307-324 in J. Dupâquier et al. (eds.) Marriage and Remarriage in Populations of the Past. New York: Academic Press.

HETHERINGTON, E. M., M. COX and R. COX (1976) "Divorced fathers." Family Coordinator 25: 417-428.

HETHERINGTON, E. M., M. COX and R. COX (1978) "The aftermath of divorce," pp. 149-176 J. H. Stevens and M. Matthews (eds.) Mother/Child, Father/Child Relations. Washington, DC: National Association for the Education of Young Children.

HOFFERTH, S. L. (1985) "Updating children's life course." Journal of Marriage and the Family 47: 93-115.

HUNTER, J. E. and N. SCHUMAN (1980) "Chronic reconstitution as a family style." Social Work 25: 446-451.

HUZAYYIN, S. A. (1981) "Marriage and remarriage in Islam," pp. 95-109 in J. Dupâquier (eds.) Marriage and Remarriage in Populations of the Past. New York: Academic Press.

IHINGER-TALLMAN, M. (1985) "Perspectives on change among stepsiblings." Presented at the annual meeting of the National Council on Family Relations, Dallas, TX.

IHINGER-TALLMAN, M. (forthcoming) "Sibling and stepsibling bonding in stepfamilies," in K. Pasley and M. Ihinger-Tallman (eds.) Remarriage and Stepparenting Today: Current Research and Theroy. New York: Guilford.

IHINGER-TALLMAN, M. and K. PASLEY (1980) "Conceptualizing marital stability: remarriage as a special case." Presented at the annual meetings of the National Council on Family Relations, Portland, OR.

IHINGER-TALLMAN, M. and K. PASLEY (1981) "Factors influencing stability in remarriage," pp. 1-15 in W. Dumon and C. De Paepe (eds.) Key Papers from the XIXth International CFS Seminar on Divorce and Remarriage. Lueven, Belgium: Catholic University.

IHINGER-TALLMAN, M. and K. PASLEY (1983) "Remarried conflict." Unpublished manuscript, Washington State University.

IMHOF, A. E. (1981) "Remarriage in rural populations and in urban middle and upper strata in Germany from the sixteenth to the twentieth century," pp. 335-346 in J. Dupâquier et al. (eds.) Marriage and Remarriage in Populations of the Past. New York: Academic Press.

ISHII-KUNTZ, M. (1986) "Sex and race differences in marital happiness of first-married and remarried persons: update and refinement." Unpublished manuscript, Washington State University.

JACOBSON, D. S. (1979) "Stepfamilies: myths and realities." Social Work 24: 202-207.

JACOBSON, D. S. (1980) "Crisis intervention with stepfamilies." New Directions for Mental Health Services 6: 35-43.

JACOBSON, D. S. (1982) Family structure in the age of divorce." Presented at the annual convention of the American Psychological Association, Washington, D.C.

JACOBSON, D. S. (forthcoming) "Family type, visiting patterns, and children's behavior in the stepfamily: a linked family system," in K. Pasley and M. Ihinger-Tallman (eds.) Remarriage and Stepparenting Today: Theory and Research. New York: Guilford.

JACOBSON, P. H. (1959) American Marriage and Divorce. New York: Rinehart.

KAPLAN, H. B. and A. D. POKORNY (1971) "Self-derogation and childhood broken home." Journal of Marriage and the Family 33: 328-337.

KARGMAN, M. W. (1969) "Legal obligations of remarriage: what is and what ought to be." Family Coordinator 18: 174-177.

KELLAM, S. G., M. E. ENSMINGER and R. J. TURNER (1977) "Family structure and the mental health of children: concurrent and longitudinal community-wide studies." Archives of General Psychiatry 34: 1012-1022.

KELLY, J. B. (1981) "The visiting relationship after divorce: research findings and clinical implications," in I. R. Stuart and L. W. Abt (eds.) Children of Separation and Divorce. New York: Van Nostrand Reinhold.

KNAUB, P. K. and S. L. HANNA (1984) "Children of remarriage: perceptions of family strengths." Journal of Divorce 7: 73-90.

KNAUB, P. K., S. L. HANNA and N. STINNETT (1984) "Strengths of remarried families." Journal of Divorce 7: 41-55.

KNOX, R. (1966). An Historical Relation of Ceylon. Ceylon: Tisara Press.

KOREN, P. E., J. I. LAHTI, C. A. SADLER and P. J. KIMBOKO (1983) The Adjustment of New Stepfamilies: Characteristics and Trends. Portland OR: Regional Research Institute for Human Services.

KRAM, S. W. and N. A. FRANK (1982) The Law of Child Custody: Development of the Substantive Law. Lexington, MA: D. C. Heath.

KRESSEL, K. (1985) The Process of Divorce: How Professionals and Couples Negotiate Settlement. New York: Basic Books.

LAGONI, L. S. and A. S. COOK (1985) "Stepfamilies: a content analysis of the popular literature, 1961-1982." Family Relations 34: 521-525.

LANDIS, P. H. (1950) "Sequential marriage." Journal of Home Economics 42: 625-628.

LANGER, T. S. and S. T. MICHAEL (1963) Life Stress and Mental Health. New York: Macmillan.

LARSON, J. H. and J. O. ANDERSON (1984) Effective Stepparenting. New York: Family Service Association of America.

LASLETT, P. (1977) Family Life and Illicit Love in Earlier Generations. Cambridge, MA: Cambridge University Press.

LEIK, R. and S. LEIK (n.d.) "The Process of commitment: behavioral continuity to relationship stability." Unpublished manuscript, University of Minnesota.

LIVI-BACCI, M. (1981) "On the frequency of remarriage in nineteenth century Italy: methods and results," pp. 347-361 in J. Dupâquier et al. (eds.) Marriage and Remarriage in Populations of the Past. New York: Academic Press.

LUEPNITZ, D. A. (1982) Child Custody: A Study of Families after Divorce. Lexington, MA: D. C. Heath.

LUTZ, P. (1983) "The stepfamily: an adolescent perspective." Family Relations 32: 367-375.

MAROTZ-BADEN, R., G. R. ADAMS, N. BUECHE, B. MUNRO and G. MUNRO (1979) "Family form or family process? Reconsidering the deficit family model approach." Family Coordinator 28: 5-14.

McCARTHY, J. (1978) "A comparison of the probability of the dissolution of first and second marriage." Demography 15: 345-359.

McCLENAHAN, C. (1978) "Group work with stepparents and their spouses." Unpublished manuscript.

MESSINGER, L. (1976) "Remarriage between divorced people with children from previous marriages: a proposal for preparation for remarriage." Journal of Marriage and Family Counseling 2: 193-200.

MESSINGER, L. (1984) Remarriage: A Family Affair. New York: Plenum.

MESSINGER, L. and K. WALKER (1981) "From marriage breakdown to remarriage: parental tasks and therapeutic guidelines." American Journal of Orthopsychiatry 51: 429-438.

MESSINGER, L., L. N. WALKER and F. J. FREEMAN (1978) "Preparation for remarriage following divorce: the use of group techniques." American Journal of Orthopsychiatry 48: 263-272.

MILLS, D. (1984) "A model for stepfamily development." Family Relations 33: 365-372.

MORGAN, S. P. and R. R. RINDFUS (1985) "Marital disruptions: structural and temporal dimensions." American Journal of Sociology 90: 1055-1077.

NADLER, J. (1976) "The psychological stress of the stepmother." Dissertation Abstracts International 37: 5367B.

OLSON, D. H., H. I. McCUBBIN, H. BARNES, A. LARSEN, M. MUXEN and M. WILSON (1983) Families: What Makes Them Work. Beverly Hills, CA: Sage.

OLSON, D. H., C. S. RUSSELL and D. H. SPRINKEL (1979) "Circumplex model of marital and family systems, I: cohesion and adaptability dimensions, family types, and clinical applications." Family Process 18: 3-28.

OSHMAN, H. P. and M. MANOSEVITZ (1976) "Father absence: effects of stepfathers upon psychosocial development in males." Developmental Psychology 12: 479-480.

PAPERNOW, P. (1984) "The stepfamily cycle: an experiential model of stepfamily development." Family Relations 33: 355-363.

PARKER, R. (1982) "Family and social policy: an overview," pp. 357-371 in R. N. Rapport, et al. (eds.) Families in Britain. London: Routledge & Kegan Paul.

PASLEY, K. (forthcoming) "Family boundary ambiguity: perspective of adult stepfamily members," in K. Pasley and M. Ihinger-Tallman (eds.) Remarriage and Stepparenting Today: Current Research and Theory. New York: Guilford.

PASLEY, K. and M. IHINGER-TALLMAN (1980) "Yours, mine and ours: remarried family life." Grand-in-aid proposal funded by Washington State University.

PASLEY, K. and M. IHINGER-TALLMAN (1985) "Portraits of stepfamily life in popular literature: 1940:1980." Family Relations 34: 527-534.

PASLEY, K. and M. IHINGER-TALLMAN (1986) "Stepfamilies: new challenges for the schools," pp. 70-111 in T. Fairchild (ed.) Crisis Intervention Strategies for School-Based Helpers. Springfield, ILL: Charles C. Thomas Publishers.

PEEK, C. W., J. L. FISCHER and J. S. KIDWELL (1985) "Teenage violence toward parents: a neglected dimension of family violence." Journal of Marriage and the Family 47: 1051-1058.

PETERSON, J. L. and N. ZILL (1986) "Marital disruption, parent-child relationships, and behavior problems in children." Journal of Marriage and the Family 48: 295-307.

PINK, J. E. and K. S. WAMPLER (1985) "Problem areas in stepfamilies: cohesion, adaptability, and the stepfather-adolescent relationship." Family Relations 34: 327-335.

PRICE-BONHAM S. and J. O. BALSWICK (1980) "The noninstitutions: divorce, desertion, and remarriage." Journal of Marriage and the Family 42: 959-972.

RAUSH, H. L., A. C. GREIF and J. NUGENT (1979) "Communication in couples and families," pp. 468-489 in W. R. Burr et al. Contemporary Theories About the Family, vol 1: Research-Based Theories, New York: Free Press.

RENNE, K. S. (1971) "Health and marital experience in an urban population." Journal of Marriage and the Family 33: 338-350.

RICCI, I. (1980) "Divorce, remarriage and the schools." Stepfamily Bulletin, 1: 2-3.

RILEY, M. W. (1982) "Families in an aging society." Paper presented at the annual meetings of National Council on Family Relations, Washington, D.C.

RISMAN, B. L. (1986) "Can men 'mother?' Life as a single father." Family Relations 35: 95-102.

ROBINSON, M. (1980) "Step-families: a reconstituted family system." Journal of Family Therapy 2: 45-69.

ROSENBERG, E. (1980) "Therapy with siblings in reorganizing families." International Journal of Family Therapy 2: 139-150.

ROSENBERG, M. (1965) Society and the Adolescent Self-Image. Princeton, NJ: Princeton University Press.

ROSS, H. E. and J. I. MILGRAM (1982) "Important variables in adult sibling relationships: a qualitative study," pp. 225-249 in M. E. Lamb and B. Sutten-Smith (eds.) Sibling Relationships: Their Nature and Significance Across the Lifespan. Hillsdale, NJ: Lawrence Erlbaum.

RUBIN, L. B. (1985) Just Friends: The Role of Friendship in Our Lives. New York: Harper & Row.

SAGER, S. J., H. STEER, H. CROHN, E. RODSTEIN and E. WALKER (1980) "Remarriage revisited." Family and Child Mental Health Journal 6: 19-33.

SANTROCK, J. W. (1972) "Relation of type and onset of father absence to cognitive development." Child Development 43: 455-469.

SANTROCK, J. W., R. WARSHAK, C. LINDBERGH and L. MEADOWS (1982) "Children's and parents' observed social behavior in stepfather families." Child Development 53: 472-480.

SCHLESINGER, B. (1970) "Remarriage as family reorganization for divorced persons: a Canadian study." Journal of Comparative Family Studies 1: 101-118.

SCHOFIELD, R. and E. A. WRIGLEY (1981) "Remarriage intervals and the effect of marriage order on fertility, pp. 211-227 in J. Dupâquier et al. (eds.) Marriage and Remarriage in Populations of the Past. New York: Academic Press.

SCHULMAN, G. L. (1972) "Myths that intrude on the adaptation of the stepfamily." Social Casework 53: 131-139.

SCHVANDEVELDT, J. D. and M. IHINGER (1979) "Sibling relationships in the family," pp. 453-467 in W. R. Burr et al. (eds.) Contemporary Theories About the Family, vol 1: Research-Based Theories. New York: Free Press.

SEWELL, W. H. and R. M. HAUSER (1975) Education, Occupation, and Earnings. New York: Academic Press.

SHAW, M. E. and P. R. COSTANZO (1970) Theories of Social Psychology. New York: McGraw-Hill.

SOGNER, S. and J. DUPÂQUIER (1981) "Introduction," pp. 1-11 in J. Dupâquier et al. (eds.) Marriage and Remarriage in Populations of the Past. New York: Academic Press.

SPANIER, G. B. (1983) "Married and unmarried cohabitation in the United States: 1980." Journal of Marriage and the Family 45: 277-288.

SPANIER, G. S. and P. C. GLICK (1981) "Marital instability in the United States: some correlates and recent changes." Family Relations 30: 329-338.

SPICER, J. W. and G. D. HAMPE (1975) "Kinship interaction after the divorce." Journal of Marriage and the Family 37: 113-119.

SPREITZER, E. and L. E. RILEY (1974) "Factors associated with singlehood." Journal of Marriage and the Family 36: 533-542.

STERN, P. N. (1978) "Stepfather families: integration around child discipline." Issues in Mental Health Nursing 1: 49-56.

STROTHER, J. and E. JACOBS (1984) Adolescent stress as it relates to stepfamily living: implications for school counselors." School Counselor 32: 97-103.

TALLMAN, I. (1976) Passion, Action, and Politics: A Perspective on Social Problems and Social-Problem Solving. San Francisco: W. H. Freeman.

TROPH, W. D. (1984) "An exploratory examination of the effects of remarriage on child support and personal contact." Journal of Divorce 7: 57-73.

VISHER, E. B. and J. S. VISHER (1978a) "Major areas of difficulty for stepparent couples." International Journal of Family Counseling 6: 70-80.

VISHER, E. B. and J. S. VISHER (1978b) "Common problems of stepparents and their spouses." American Journal of Orthopsychiatry 48: 252-262.

VISHER, E. B. and J. S. VISHER (1979) Stepfamilies: A Guide to Working With Stepparent and Stepchildren. New York: Brunner/Mazel.

VISHER, E. B. and J. S. VISHER (forthcoming) "Treating families with problems associated with remarriage and step-relationships," in C. Chilman et al. (eds.) Families in Trouble. Beverly Hills, CA: Sage.

WALD, E. (1981) The Remarried Family: Challenge and Promise. New York: Family Service Association of America.

WALKER, K. N. and L. MESSINGER (1979) "Remarriage after divorce: dissolution and construction of family boundaries." Family Process 18: 185-192.

WALLERSTEIN, J. S. and J. B. KELLEY (1980) Surviving the Break-Up: How Children and Parents Cope with Divorce. New York: Basic Books.

WALSH, L. S. (1977) "Charles County, Maryland, 1658-1705: a study in Chesapeake political and social structure." Doctoral dissertation, Michigan State University.

WEINGARTEN, H. R. (1980) "Remarriage and well-being: national survey evidence of social and psychological effects." Journal of Family Issues 1: 533-559.

WEISS, R. S. (1975) Marital Separation. New York: Basic Books.

WEISS, R. S. (1979) Going It Alone. New York: Basic Books.

WEITZMAN, L. (1985) The Divorce Revolution: The Unexpected Social and Economic Consequences for Women and Children in America. New York: Free Press.

WHITE, L. K. (1979) "Sex differentials in the effect of remarriage on global happiness." Journal of Marriage and the Family 41: 869-876.

WHITE, L. K. and A. BOOTH (1985) "The quality and stability of remarriages: the role of stepchildren." American Sociological Review 50: 689-698.

WHITESIDE, M. F. (1981) "A family systems approach with families of remarriage,"
    pp. 319-337 in I. R. Stuart and L. E. Abt (eds.) Children of Separation and Divorce.
    New York: Van Nostrand Reinhold.
WILLIAMS, F. R. and L. K. O'HERN (1979) "Second time around: relationship in
    second marriages." Presented at the annual meeting of the National Council on Family
    Relations, Boston, MA.
WILSON, K. L., L. A. ZURCHER, D. C. MacADAMS and R. L. CURTIS (1975) "Step-
    fathers and stepchildren: an exploratory analysis from two national surveys." Jour-
    nal of Marriage and the Family, 37: 526-536.
WOLF, A. B. (1981) "Women, widowhood and fertility in pre-modern China," pp.
    139-147 in J. Dupâquier et al. (eds.) Marriage and Remarriage in Populations of
    the Past. New York: Academic Press.

Author Index

Subject Index

Abuse: directed against children, 56; directed against parents, 56; in folk tales, 78

Adjustment of children to remarriage: academic achievement in children, 89; behavior problems, 92; cognitive functioning in children, 89; factors influencing, 87, 88; psychological functioning, 89, 90; self-esteem, self-confidence, and personality variables, 89; sex differences in, 88

Adoption, 126

Anticipatory socialization, 120

Attachment: of children to stepfamily, 55; between former spouses, 17, 73; between stepsiblings, 105, 106, 107

Binuclear family: affect between former spouses, 45; and boundary maintenance, 54, 55, 56; child comparisons, 92; community support, 125; definition of, 43; as typology, 47; and visitation, 82

Blended families: see Stepfamily terminology

Charivaris, 25, 26, 29

Child shifting: see Custody

Child in common, 47, 104

Cohabitation, 60

Cohesion: definition of, 52; disrupted by children, 93; as family process, 50; time to develop, 52

Cohort, 17, 21, 30, 36

Colonial America, 33

Commitment: children's commitment, 50-51; as family process, 50-51; in marriage vs. cohabitation, 17; as part of models of stepfamily adjustment, 117; to make policy changes, 124; among remarried spouses, 50-51; reasons for lack of commitment, 51; of researchers to be theoretical, 139

Common pot vs. two pot pattern of financial distribution, 70

Communication: factors that affect communication, 53; improved through premarital education experience, 119; and marital problems, 62; and marital stability, 68; quality of, 53-54; in stepfather families, 92, 100; in stepmother families, 102-103; strategies for developing communication, 118

Conflict: apparent in developmental stages, 122; areas of conflict in remarriage, 63; children affected by, 19-20; over child support, 85; and cohesion, 52; and communication, 53; over discipline of children, 93-94; over ex-spouse, 17-18; over finances, 71, 100; reduced through educational program, 120; with relatives, 99; over resource distribution, 69-71; in stepmothers, 101-102; between stepparent-stepchild, 101, 119; between stepsiblings, 108, 109

Conjugal succession, 21

Contact: with biological mother, 103; child-father, 82-83, 84, 95; between former spouses, 43, 46; frequency of contact, 50; with helping agencies and community organizations, 67; new spouse's influence on, 83; quality of contact, 46; as stage in stepfamily development, 122; with therapist, 122; as variable in typology, 47

Custody, 19, 95; "best interests of the child" doctrine, 79, 80; cooperative parenting, 47; custody changes, 85-86, 95; effects of no-fault divorce legislation, 82; history of, 79-82; joint custody, 47, 79, 81-82, 83, 84; "parental rights" doctrine, 79; reasons for custody change, 86; reasons for paternal custody, 99; sole custody, 86; split custody, 47;

About the Authors

Marilyn Ihinger-Tallman is Associate Professor of Sociology at Washington State University. She received her Ph.D. in Sociology from the University of Minnesota in 1977. Her research and writing have centered on remarriage, stepparenting, and sibling socialization. In collaboration with Kay Pasley she helped organize the Focus Group on Remarriage and Stepparenting, sponsored by the National Council on Family Relations, coedited a special issue of *Family Relations* on remarriage and stepparenting (July 1984), and organized the Study Group on the Influence of Remarriage and Stepparenting on Child Development and the Quality of Family Life, sponsored by the Society for Research in Child Development. She is currently planning a study on commitment and bonding among siblings and stepsiblings.

Kay Pasley is Associate Professor of Human Development and Family Studies at Colorado State University. She received her Ed.D. degree from Indiana University in 1974 in early childhood education, child development, and family life. For several years she has been actively engaged in investigating the dynamics of remarriage and stepfamily living. She is the author and coauthor of articles and book chapters on these topics and is currently studying the influence of financial management practices on family functioning among remarried couples.

DATE DUE

8/24/88			

DEMCO 38-297